The Proper Care of
GERMAN SHEPHERDS

TW-144

Facing Page: An excellent example of an American-bred German Shepherd Dog. Courtesy of James Moses.

The portrayal and discussion of canine pet products in this book are for instructive value only and do not necessarily constitute an endorsement by the author, publisher, or the owners of dogs depicted in this book.

Photographers: Alverson Photographers, Inc.; Ashbey Photography; Licia Babb; Nancy and Carmelo Battaglia; Jim and Bobbie Cusick; Tara Darling; Isabelle Francais; Mary Gattone; Jim Hall; Corinna Kamer, Kaven Kierst; Max Lee; Cathy Mekula; James Moses; Ceila Ooi; Gina Ostroman; Robert Pearcy; Norman J. Seldes; Vince Serbin; Dan and Sandra Smith; Robert Smith; Elena Stangel; Judith E. Strom; Susan Sullivan; Karen Taylor; Van Cleve Kennels; Al and Karen Wagner.

The author acknowledges the contribution of fellow German Shepherd enthusiast, Christine Walkowicz for the chapters: "Prevention and Cure," "Showing Your Dog," and "Let's Play Ball!"

Distributed in the UNITED STATES to the Pet Trade by T.F.H. Publications, Inc., One T.F.H. Plaza, Neptune City, NJ 07753; distributed in the UNITED STATES to the Bookstore and Library Trade by National Book Network, Inc. 4720 Boston Way, Lanham MD 20706; in CANADA to the Pet Trade by H & L Pet Supplies, Inc., 27 Kingston Crescent, Kitchener, Ontario N2B 2T6; Rolf C. Hagen Inc., 3225 Sartelon St. Laurent-Montreal Quebec H4R 1E8; in CANADA to the Book Trade by Vanwell Publishing Ltd., 1 Northrup Crescent, St. Catharines, Ontario L2M 6P5 ; in ENGLAND by T.F.H. Publications, PO Box 15, Waterlooville PO7 6BQ; in AUSTRALIA AND THE SOUTH PACIFIC by T.F.H. (Australia), Pty. Ltd., Box 149, Brookvale 2100 N.S.W., Australia; in NEW ZEALAND by Brooklands Aquarium Ltd. 5 McGiven Drive, New Plymouth, RD1 New Zealand; in Japan by T.F.H. Publications, Japan—Jiro Tsuda, 10-12-3 Ohjidai, Sakura, Chiba 285, Japan; in SOUTH AFRICA by Lopis (Pty) Ltd., P.O. Box 39127, Booysens, 2016, Johannesburg, South Africa. Published by T.F.H. Publications, Inc.
MANUFACTURED IN THE
UNITED STATES OF AMERICA
BY T.F.H. PUBLICATIONS, INC.

The Proper Care of
GERMAN SHEPHERDS

by Dr. Carmelo L. Battaglia

Ch. Cobert's Smokescreen, "Paige," owned by Cathy Mekula.

Contents

Ch. G.V. Sukee's Mannix ROM owned by Jim and Bobbie Cusick.

Acknowledgments

Anyone who writes a book about the German Shepherd Dog must sooner or later admit that his knowledge and what he has written are possible only with the help of others. I am no exception to the rule. Since 1990, I have gathered information, materials and photos for this book. My efforts have required the help and aid of many friends, breeders, researchers, authors and the staff of the American Kennel Club. Without their

The stance of the German Shepherd Dog makes him unique from all other breeds. The extended hind leg shows the correct angle of the hock (ankle) and the flow of the topline (along the back). This is Am.–Can. Select Ch. Survival D'Artagnon Stormfield owned by Betty Ogren.

Ch. Cobert's Smokescreen bred and owned by Cathy Mekula.

President of the Verin fur Deutsche Schaferhund, S.V. and Mr. Lux, its long-time director. While studying the breed during my trips to Germany, Austria and Holland, I was fortunate to have as my personal liaison Mrs. Anne Due, the representative from the German Shepherd Dog Club of America who resides in Germany. Her work and contacts, coupled with her role as my interpreter, were invaluable.

Thanks are also due to Dr. Al Corley of the OFA and "Scootie" Helen Sherlock, a dear colleague, for their valuable correspondence and phone calls about many health issues and structural improvements in the

cooperation, help and assistance, this book could not have been written.

The involvement of the breed from the prespective of the Germans was possible with the help of Mr. Hermann Martin,

breed. Standards are published by permission of the American Kennel Club and the Verin fur Deutsche Schaferhund, S.V.

Many thanks to my wife Nancy for her timeless editing and, last but not least my friends and colleagues for their cooperation and the photos submitted for this publication.

Seven-week-old Epic's Feature Presentation, "Kate", owned by Cathy Mekula.

Introduction

This is a book about the German Shepherd Dog, or the Alsatian as it was formerly called in England. It is the most recognizable dog in the world and the breed that serves

The German Shepherd Dog is very versatile and intelligent; it ranks among the most trainable of breeds.

as the standard for the working abilities in the canine. So much has been accomplished with this dog that countries have used it in every aspect of their society. It is truly "man's best friend."

The literature dates back to the 1800s, and since then there has been a steady stream of books and articles praising the German Shepherd's usage and worth. When writers have attempted to study the breed they have been overwhelmed by the magnitude of what has been reported and its accomplishments in time of war and peace. The main problem with most books about dogs is that they tell about things that people already know about. Emphasis usually is placed on a few notable dogs, followed by chapters on how to feed and raise them which is then followed by a long and impressive list of champions in the breed. This book is more than the compilation of what is known about the important German Shepherds.

Jeck Vom Noricum German Sieger 1993. The German Shepherd Dog is arguably the most recognizable dog in the world.

History of the German Shepherd

ORIGIN IN GERMANY

History shows that the canine species has been part of the human life experience for 70 thousand years. Cave paintings depict dogs working and tending sheep for humans. The canines described in these paintings were usually the same: a curled, heavily haired tail, erect ears like those of a Husky, a coat like a German Shepherd, and always as the companion of man. In the diverse sections of the European continent, dogs were found to be best suited to work with shepherds. On the northern flatlands of Germany, a light-footed dog that could trot for many hours developed. It was selected for the job to work in both the mountain and central regions of Germany. Within a short time the best herding dogs, a crude kind of animal, developed because of its utilitarian type dense coat and versatility.

Selection was based on those that worked the best. Over time, this special dog began

The erect ears and wedge-shaped muzzle of the German Shepherd are celebrated hallmarks of the breed.

to be improved and recognized for its working and herding skills.

THE FIRST GERMAN SHEPHERD DOG

The Verein fur Deutsche Schaferhunde, S.V., is the national German Dog Club. It was the life work of Rittmeister von Stephanitz and came into being almost by chance on April 3, 1899. On that day von Stephanitz and his close friend and associate Arthur Meyer while in Karlsruhe, a city in western Germany, attended one of the first all-breed shows ever held. As they were walking through the crowds noticing different dogs, being critical but dispassionate, they came to notice one that was different. He was a medium-sized, yellow and grey wolf-like dog standing quietly next to his handler. Both men had been interested in the native shepherd dogs because of their outstanding herding abilities, which they had observed in Wurtemberg, Thuringia, and Saxony. Neither had seen such an outstanding example of the Shepherd breed as this one. They carefully examined him and concluded that this dog was the primal canine type, uncorrupted by the influence of man. He was agile, powerful and appeared to have great endurance, steadiness, alertness and intelligence. On questioning the handler, they learned that the dog was not used would direct and polish his skills.

The inborn desire and ability to serve, along with his wolfish

Today's German Shepherd Dog embodies the old shepherd dog prototype and is ideally suited for the task of herding.

as a show dog, but as a working shepherd born with these natural abilities, thus requiring little training other than some early socialization, and then later some training that appearance, made him a unique specimen. It was the dog that would become the corner post of the breed. This dog's name was Hektor von Linksrhein.

The interbreeding of three ancient strains of European Shepherd dog was supervised by von Stephanitz. The results of this effort was a distinctive blend of intelligence and beauty.

Arthur Meyer and von Stephanitz envisioned in Hektor the possibilities of the future. In this one dog they saw the answer to all of their dreams. He was the ideal type with the temperament and character needed to become the first registered German Shepherd Dog. On that day, with little fan fare, and no preparation, they formed the Verin fur Deutsche Schaferhunde, S.V.

Hektor von Linksrhein was purchased by von Stephanitz and renamed Horand von Grafrath and registered as the first German Shepherd Dog. His registration number was S.Z.1.

In the words of von Stephanitz, "Horand embodied for the enthusiasts of that time the fulfillment of their dreams." He was big for that period, between 24" and 24 $^1/_2$" at the wither. He was the dog destined to shape the breed because of his type, coat, temperament, and color. Most other dogs from the region were coarse, wiry, small, stocky, wolf-grey in color with pricked or standing ears. During the first days of this organization their efforts and their goals were aimed toward fixing the base and shaping the breed so it could be better developed. Their early efforts began with a search for dogs, especially bitches that had produced types similar to Horand's. When one was found and it was determined that she could produce the desired type, she was purchased and care-

Puppies inherit structure as well as temperament from their sire and dam; it is therefore important to observe the parents of the pup before you make your selection.

1996 Best of Maturity winner, Ch. Sharobis Quik Legend, "Ree."

fully inbred. One of these early bitches, Freya von Grafrath, registration number S.Z.7, was bred to Horand four times.

While Horand would go on to sire many litters the most important of his get would be Hektor von Schwaben. Hektor, produced three great sons, Beowulf, Heinz von Starkenburg, and Pilot III. This great triumvirate would influence generations for years to come. Beowulf was a great producer of bitches. Pilot III, through his grandson Graf Eberhard von Hohen-Esp, produced the foundation stock for the von Boll and Kriminalpolizei strains. Heinz von Starkenburg became the most important of the three.

On November 1, 1903, a litter was whelped by Bella von Starkenburg, and sired by Heinz von Starkenburg. In this litter there was a solid black puppy considered by von Stephanitz and others to be the model for the breed. He was a vast improvement over other stud dogs of his time. This young black dog was named Roland von

Starkenburg and was used to demonstrate the effective use of close breeding.

Roland became the model for the breed because in this one animal, a vast genetic improvement had occurred. From the first German Shepherd Dog (Horand), the breed made a vast improvement in just four generations with the occurrence and prepotency of Roland. Horand's greatest son, Hektor had produced three sons (Beowulf,

Most German Shepherd breeders of the past found that concentrating their care and attention on a few dogs produced better results than raising the dogs on a larger scale.

Pilot III and Heinz), the third son, Heinz produced the genetic agent for the breed, he was called Roland.

It is no surprise that these important pillars of the breed also became the most important dogs during the first Sieger shows as is illustrated below.

List of Early German Siegers and Siegerians:

Roland's best-known son, Hettel Uckermark, became Sieger in 1909. He sired many great offspring including the International Grand Champion of 1920. The next key dog and breed pillar in the chain of great dogs was Klodo v. Boxberg, who had been the Czechoslovakian Sieger in 1923. He was a different type from those before him who were taller, and somewhat square. Klodo was lower stationed, deeper in body, and longer than others before him. He was gray and tan, beautifully proportioned, with a magnificent outline. He possessed a firm body and had a fearless character.

At the German Sieger show, von Stephanitz, serving as president and also the master judge, as was the custom, motioned for Klodo, who was in third place, to move into second place. After further consideration and competition, in a dramatic move, he gestured with a sweep of his arm for this great animal to move into first place.

This decision declared Klodo triumphant and the new World's Sieger.

Possessing one of the most expressive faces in the canine world, the German Shepherd Dog is a reliable, trustworthy, and gracious friend.

THE GERMAN SHEPHERD CLUB IN AMERICA

The first German Shepherd Dogs in this country were entered in shows as German Sheepdogs. In 1911, they were registered by the American Kennel Club as a separate breed; in 1918, the AKC listed them as Shepherd Dogs and in 1930, the name became German Shepherd Dog. Appar-

German Shepherds are an active breed and need plenty of freedom to maintain their well-muscled, limber appearance.

ently the first bitch to enter America was Mira v. Offingen (Beowulf x Hella v. Schwaben) who was imported in 1906. She was shown in 1907, 1908, and again in 1913.

The first champion of the breed occurred on July 13, 1913, Ch. Herta v. Ehrangrund. The German Shepherd Dog Club of America was organized in 1913 by Miss Anne Tracy and Benjamin Throop, and incorporated in the State of New York in 1916 as a non-profit organization. The charter members were Anne Tracy, Mrs. S. C. Eristoff, Margaret C. Throop, Edith Mae Schley, Vernon Castle, John Volkman, Paul Huhn and R. B.

Ruggles. The first magazine was called the *BULLETIN* and later *THE SHEPHERD DOG*. Today, the breed magazine is called the *German Shepherd Dog REVIEW*, which is sent monthly to all members of the parent club.

This is one of only a few breeds whose name includes the word "Dog." In England, because of the first World War with the Germans, the breed name was changed to "Alsatian." By 1978, the mood of the country had changed and the name was changed back to the German Shepherd Dog.

As a breed, the German Shepherd Dog is said to have no equal in its ability to perform a wide variety of func-

German Shepherds have a reputation of being noble and reliable. They are often used as Seeing Eye™ dogs for the blind.

tions. It has been used in service to mankind in more ways than any other breed because of its reliability, versatility and willingness to work.

Its use as the "Seeing Eye" for thousands of blind persons is well known because of the focus on its intelligence, loyalty and dependability. With the Armed Services it was selected because of its alertness, trainability, keen scent and endurance. The civil authorities have found the breed useful in many ways because of the breed's adaptability and courage. The general public likes the breed for its companionship, sensitivity, responsiveness, devotion, trustworthiness, beauty and protection.

The German Shepherd's superior intelligence, strength, and endurance have made him popular among the police and military.

The German Shepherd Dog Club of America (GSDCA) is an organization dedicated to the improvement of the breed. Membership includes breeders, fanciers, trainers and handlers who are devoted to the breed. The GSDCA is a member of the American Kennel Club, (AKC) an organization of all-breed and specialty clubs which maintains the registration of pure bred dogs in what is called the stud book. When World War I began with Germany, the name was changed to the Shepherd Club of America. It was not until 1994 that the club discovered that the name had never

Intelligent and aware, the German Shepherd makes an excellent companion and protector.

been officially changed, and in 1995 the name was changed back to the German Shepherd Dog Club of America, Inc.

Throughout the United States there are over 120 local German Shepherd Dog clubs (regional clubs) that are recognized by the German Shepherd Dog Club of America (GSDCA). National clubs like the GSDCA are commonly called "parent clubs" because they provide guidance and assistance to the breed, public, and fancy as well as to the regional clubs. The first national specialty show held just for German Shepherd Dogs was in 1918, and the first winner of the national show was Ch. Komet v. Hoheluft. The German Shepherds that win this prestigious show are called the Best of Breed and Best of Opposite Sex, and they are considered to be the national champions. The GSDCA also gives these winners special honorary titles. Until 1925, they were called the Grand Champions, thereafter, the winners were called the Grand Victor/Victrix (GV). The males and females that are the runners-up to the Grand Victor and Grand Victrix are called the Select Dogs and the Select Bitches. In 1932, no Grand Victor title was awarded by the judge of the national, who was from Germany, because he felt that none of the entries were worthy of the title. Again in 1936, no Grand Victor title was awarded for the same reason.

REGIONAL CLUBS

There are over 120 regional German Shep-

Your German Shepherd will thrive with any type of outdoor exercise. This German Shepherd is enjoying a romp in the snow.

herd Dog clubs in the United States with a membership of over four thousand. In Canada and in the United States, regional clubs have regular monthly meetings, offer educational programs and newsletters, and sponsor fun matches, sweepstakes and specialty shows.

According to the AKC records for 1994, German Shepherds again ranked in the top ten in popularity among the 130 registered breeds. By

Schutzhund training is not the same as attack training. Schutzhund involves a high degree of skill used over a variety of activities. Sleeve work is but one of the many levels of Schutzhund work.

comparison, for the year 1994, the AKC reported that the American public registered 77,000 puppies to over 65,000 individuals, the Canadian Kennel Club registered 7,000 German Shepherd Dogs and the S.V. registered 20,000. In all three countries, most of the German Shepherds are used as companions although there are growing numbers each year of dogs being used to compete in performance events such as herding, tracking, obedience, and agility trials.

WORLD COMPETITION

The most complex and interesting of all world sports for dogs are those involving performance activities. In most countries the sport is called Schutzhund. It is a three-part activity involving tracking, obedience and protection work.

The German Shepherd Dog is well-suited for this sport because of its versatility and willingness to work. Dogs selected for this sport must have good nerves and working abilities or they will not score high. Much of the competition places emphasis on the dog's concentration, willingness to work, ability to discriminate, and respond with and without commands from the handler. Dogs trained for this sport thrive on rewards and reinforcement to produce an outstanding performance.

The AKC approves shows and matches for the all-breed clubs and for specialty clubs. Most clubs host two shows and two fun matches each year. Matches are used by members to teach their pups the art of what is expected in the show and obedience ring. They are called fun matches because it is a time for families to picnic and have the fun of showing their eager pups.

GERMANY

The German Shepherd Dog Club of Germany is called the

Farah Von Nordrstein owned by Ruth Zieleniewski.

Verein fur Deutsche Schaferhunde, S.V. It serves as the center point for the breed because it was the country where the breed originated. It is the place where competition is at its best. Germany is about the size of the state of Georgia and the place where the German Shepherd is considered the national dog. Dog clubs throughout most of Europe are civic organizations that meet many of the social needs of their members. Dogs are often kenneled at their club headquarters, which are generally owned by the local club. Many are housed on one or more acres. These sites provide a nightly place for members to meet, train, and socialize.

STANDARD OF THE BREED

The AKC standard and the one used throughout Europe have slight differences. The most notable difference between the two is in the length of the body and the amount of desired angulation. As you read the standards notice that the German-bred dog is not as long in body as the American bred dog. For your reference, here is the American Kennel Club Standard for the German Shepherd Dog.

AKC BREED STANDARD
General Appearance— The first impression of a good

German Shepherd Dog is that of a strong, agile, well-muscled animal, alert and full of life. It is well balanced, with harmonious development of the forequarter and hindquarter. The dog is longer than tall, deep bodied, and presents an outline of smooth curves rather than angles. It looks substantial and not spindly, giving the impression, both at rest and in motion, of muscular firmness and nimbleness without any look of clumsiness or soft living. The ideal dog is stamped with a look of quality and nobil-

1982 Grand Victor Ch. Kismet's Impulse von Bismark.

The ideal German Shepherd Dog is stamped with a look of quality and nobility that is difficult to define but unmistakable when present.

ninity, according to its sex.

Size, Proportion, Substance— The desired **height** for males at the top of the highest point of the shoulder blade is 24 to 26 inches; and for bitches, 22-24 inches. The German Shepherd Dog is longer than tall, with the most desirable **proportion** as 10 to 8 $1/2$. The length is measured from the point of the prosternum or breastbone to the rear edge of the pelvis, the ischial tuberosity. The desirable long proportion is not derived from a long back, but from overall length with relation to height, which is achieved by length of forequarter and length of withers and hindquarter,

ity—difficult to define, but unmistakable when present. Secondary sex characteristics are strongly marked, and every animal gives a definite impression of masculinity or femi-

viewed from the side.

Head—The **head** is noble, cleanly chiseled, strong without coarseness, but above all not fine, and in proportion to the body. The head of the male is distinctly masculine, and that of the bitch distinctly feminine. The **expression** keen, intelligent and composed. **Eyes** of medium size, almond shaped, set a little obliquely and not protruding. The color is as dark as possible. **Ears** are moderately pointed, in proportion to the skull, open toward the front, and

The German Shepherd is longer than tall with the desired proportion being 10 to 8. The length is measured from the breast bone to the rear edge of the pelvis.

carried erect when at attention the ideal carriage being one in which the center lines of the ears, viewed from the front, are parallel to each other and perpendicular to the ground. A dog with cropped or hanging ears must be *disqualified.* Seen from the front, the forehead is only moderately arched, and the **skull** slopes into the long, wedge-shaped muzzle without abrupt stop. The **muzzle** is long and strong, and its topline is parallel to the topline of the skull. **Nose** black. A dog with a nose that is not predominantly black must be *disqualified.* The lips are firmly fitted. Jaws are strongly developed.

Teeth— 42 in number—20 upper and 22 lower—are strongly developed and meet in a scissors bite in which part of the inner surface of the upper incisors meet and engage part of the outer surface of the lower incisors. An overshot jaw or a level bite is undesirable. An undershot jaw is a *disqualifying fault.* Complete dentition is to be preferred. Any missing teeth other than first premolars is a *serious fault.*

Neck, Topline, Body— The **neck** is strong and muscular, clean-cut and relatively long, proportionate in size to the head and without loose folds of skin. When the dog is at attention or excited, the head is raised and the neck carried high; otherwise typical carriage of the head is forward rather than up and little higher than the top of the shoulders, particularly in motion. **Topline**— The **withers** are higher than and sloping into the level back. The **back** is straight, very strongly developed without sag or roach, and relatively short. The whole structure of the **body** gives an impression of depth and solidity without bulkiness. **Chest**— Commencing at the

The number one show dog of all time is Ch. Altana's Mystique owned by Jane A. Firestone and handled by James Moses, Judge Dr. Carmen Battaglia.

prosternum, it is well filled and carried well down between the legs. It is deep and capacious, never shallow, with ample room for lungs and heart, carried well forward, with the prosternum showing ahead of the shoulder in profile.

Ribs well sprung and long, neither barrel-shaped nor too flat, and carried down to a sternum which reaches to the elbows. Correct ribbing allows the elbows to move back freely when the dog is at a trot. Too round causes interference

Ch. Destino's Serge, owned by Mary Gattone winning Best of Breed at an outdoor show.

and throws the elbows out; too flat or short causes pinched elbows. Ribbing is carried well back so that the loin is relatively short. **Abdomen** firmly held and not paunchy. The bottom line is only moderately tucked up in the loin. **Loin**— Viewed from the top, broad and strong. Undue length between the last rib and the thigh, when viewed from the side, is undesirable. **Croup** long and gradually sloping. **Tail** bushy, with the last vertebra extended at least to the hock joint. It is set smoothly into the croup and low rather than high. At rest, the tail hangs in a slight curve like a saber. A slight hook—some-

No German Shepherd Dog is perfect when compared to the breed standard, though each dog has certain features that when viewed individually are flawless.

times carried to one side—is faulty only to the extent that it mars general appearance. When the dog is excited or in motion, the curve is accentuated and the tail raised, but it should never be curled forward beyond a vertical line. Tails too short, or with clumpy ends due to ankylosis, are *serious faults*. A dog with a docked tail must be *disqualified*.

Forequarters— The shoulder blades are long and obliquely angled, laid on flat and not placed forward. The upper arm joins the shoulder blade at about a right angle. Both the upper arm and the shoulder blade are well muscled. The forelegs, viewed from all sides, are straight and the bone oval rather than round. The pasterns are strong and springy and angulated at approximately a 25 degree angle from the vertical. Dewclaws on the forelegs may be removed, but are normally left on. The *feet* are short, compact with toes well arched, pads thick and firm, nails short and dark.

Hindquarters— The whole assembly of the thigh, viewed from the side, is broad with both upper and lower thigh well muscled, forming as nearly as possible a right angle. The upper thigh bone parallels the shoulder blade while the lower thigh bone parallels the upper arm. The metatarsus (the unit between the hock joint and the foot) is short, strong and tightly articulated. The dewclaws, if any, should be removed from the hind legs. Feet as in front.

Coat— The ideal dog has a double coat of medium length. The outer coat should be as dense as possible, hair straight, harsh and lying close to the body. A slightly wavy outer coat, often of wiry texture, is permissible.

The head, including the inner ear and foreface, and the legs and paws are covered with short hair, and the neck with longer and thicker hair. The rear of the forelegs and hind legs has somewhat longer hair extending to the pasterns and hock, respectively. *Faults* in the coat include soft, silky, too long outer coat, woolly, curly and open coat.

Color— The German Shepherd Dog varies in color, and most colors are permissible. Strong rich colors are preferred. Pale,

Ch. Covy-Tucker Hill's Manhattan, owned by Shirlee Braunstein and Jane A. Firestone, won Best in Show at the famous Westminster Kennel Club in 1987—the only breed member to accomplish this feat.

The German Shepherd Dog is well muscled, an athlete whose body structure is designed for endurance.

washed-out colors and blues or livers are *serious faults*. A white dog must be *disqualified*.

Gait— A German Shepherd Dog and its structure has been developed to meet the requirements of its work. ***General Impression—*** The gait is outreaching, elastic, seemingly without effort, smooth and rhythmic, covering the maximum amount of ground with the minimum number of steps. At a walk it covers a great deal of ground, with long strides of both hind legs and forelegs. At a trot the dog covers still more ground with even longer stride, and moves powerfully but easily, with coordination and balance so that the gait appears to be the steady motion of a well-lubricated machine. The feet travel close to the ground on both forward reach and backward push. In order to achieve movement of this kind, there must be good muscular development and ligamentation. The hindquarters deliver, through the back, a powerful forward thrust which slightly lifts the whole animal and drives the body forward. Reaching far under, and passing the imprint left by the front foot, the hind foot takes hold of the ground; then hock, stifle and upper thigh come into play and

At full trot, the German Shepherd's back must remain firm and level. The feet are brought inward toward the middle line of the body without crossing over or striking together.

The German Shepherd's coat is medium in length and as dense as possible, harsh but lying close to the body.

the normal straight line. **Transmission—** The typical smooth, flowing gait is maintained with great strength and firmness of the back. The whole effort of the hindquarter is transmitted to the forequarter through the loin, back and withers. At full trot, the back must remain firm and level without sway, roll, whip or roach. Unlevel topline with withers lower than the hip is a *fault*. To compensate for the forward motion imparted by the hindquarters, the shoulder should open to its full extent. The forelegs should reach out close to the ground in a long stride in harmony with that of the

sweep back, the stroke of the hind leg finishing with the foot still close to the ground in a smooth follow-through. The over-reach of the hind-quarter usually necessitates one hind foot passing outside and the other hindfoot passing inside the track of the forefeet, and such action is not faulty unless the locomotion is crabwise with the dog's body sideways out of hindquarters. The dog does not track on widely separated parallel lines, but brings the feet inward toward the middle line of the body when trotting, in order to maintain balance. The feet track closely but do not strike or cross over. Viewed from the front, the front legs function from the shoulder joint to the pad in a straight line. Viewed from the rear, the hind legs function from the hip joint to the pad in a straight line. Faults of gait, whether from front, rear, or side, are to be considered *very serious faults*.

Temperament— The breed has a distinct personality marked by direct and fearless, but not hostile, expression, self-confidence and a certain aloofness that does not lend itself to immediate and indiscriminate friendships. The dog must be approachable, quietly standing its ground and showing confidence and willingness to meet overtures without itself making them. It is

The German Shepherd's head is noble and cleanly chiseled; the expression is keen, intelligent and composed.

poised, but when the occasion demands, eager and alert; both fit and willing to serve in its capacity as companion, watchdog, blind leader, herding dog, or guardian, whichever the circumstances may demand. The dog must not be timid, shrinking behind its master or handler; it should not be nervous, looking about or upward with anxious expression or showing nervous reactions, such as tucking of tail, to strange sounds or sights. Lack of confidence under any surroundings is not typical of good character. Any of the above deficiencies in character which indicate shyness must be penalized as *very serious faults* and any dog exhibiting pronounced indications of these must be excused from the ring. It must be possible for the judge to observe the teeth and to determine that both testicles are descended. Any dog that attempts to bite the judge must be *disqualified*. The ideal dog is a working animal with an incorruptible character combined with body and gait suitable for the arduous work that constitutes its primary purpose.

Disqualifications

Cropped or hanging ears.
Dogs with noses not predominantly black.
Undershot jaw.
Docked tail.
White dogs.
Any dog that attempts to bite the judge.

WORLD TRIALS

Each year, teams from more than 40 countries compete to determine which German Shepherds are the best in the world. Each country is allowed to bring a team of up to seven dogs with their handlers. The GSDCA WDA was formed to interest those breeders and exhibitors who want to compete and test the working abilities of their dogs. The GSDCA team represents the US at World Trials. The site of the competition is decided yearly at the world meeting of delegates. The 1992 trial was held in Austria; the 1993 trial in Holland; the 1994 in Czechoslovakia; and the 1995 trial in Hungary. It was never held in the United States until the Boston, Massachusetts trial in 1998.

More than any other breed, the German Shepherd Dog has excelled in every task it has set out to accomplish.

This German Shepherd Dog is successfully clearing the hurdle at an obedience trial.

Each year the dogs are tested in tracking, obedience and protection. Each event is scored separately with up to 100 points being awarded for each event. At the end of the trial, teams are ranked based on the average scores earned by their dogs. Individual dogs are ranked based on their individual performance. Usually the best dogs will have point totals of 295 or better out of a possible 300 points.

GERMAN METHODS OF SHOWING AND TESTING

In 1992, the S.V. registered 28,000 German Sheperd puppies from a membership of 100,000. The German system divides the country into 20 regions (Landesgruppen) with 1500 S.V. clubs (Ortsgruppen). The S.V. membership is slightly over 100,000 individuals. Because the German Shepherd is used primarily for family activities, the S.V. offers programs to meet the needs of its

Although less frequently seen, solid black German Shepherd Dogs possess all the same charms and talents of their sable and black and tan brethren.

German Shepherd Dogs prove themselves in many rings of competition; they are highly trainable and enjoy the spotlight.

three large and diverse membership categories:

1. Young families with children.

2. Hard core breeders and handlers.

3. An older population whose members are committed to the breed but are no longer active in showing their dogs.

The best programs used by the S.V. to improve the breed have primarily been voluntary. Certification of sound dogs for their hips is a good example. While it is not a requirement to have certified hips to become a Select Dog and receive an excellent rating at the Seiger show, most exhibitors only show dogs that have the "A" stamp for sound hips.

Judges' Training

Conformation judges (Zuchtrichter) and working trial judges (Leistungsgrichter) are given training which includes a thorough understanding of tracking, obedience, and courage testing. The benefits from such an idea are seen in the consistency and reliability of their judging program. Separate symposiums designed to train and upgrade skills are held once each year. All of the S.V. judges meet with the veterinarians to discuss what problems have been observed in the past year. At these meetings they agree on what traits or characteristics need to be emphasized by the specialty judges during the next year or two. Their strategy is to inform and recommend so that judges can place emphasis on the problems they noticed.

The function of regional and local clubs is clearly defined in Germany and throughout Europe. Control and direction begins with the S.V. and disseminates through their Landesgruppen (regional club) down to their S.V. member or local clubs (Ortsgruppen). Each club has a breed warden who visits each litter no later than three days after birth, and returns at least three times for inspection of the litter during

Westminster Kennel Club judges writing down the Best in Show winner. Westminster is the most prestigious show in the United States and was won by a German Shepherd Dog in 1987.

the next several weeks. The designated S.V. tattooers, together with the breed warden, tattoo the registration number in one ear. The registration number appears on the pedigree, x-ray, breed survey, and on all of the dog's training reports. If the litter is greater than six pups, a foster mother must be used to nurse the excess pups.

The term "Select" has a common definition in Europe and throughout the world. The single exception is in the United States. The Select award in other countries is given at their national show to those dogs that rank highest who also have

Socialization is important to the development of puppies. The process should begin at a young age between the pup and his littermates.

the "A" stamp for a hip diagnosis of normal. In Germany, it is not a requirement for the parents of select dogs to have the "A" stamp, but in practice, judges do not award select ratings unless both parents also have an "A" stamp.

According to Dr. Brass, the noted authority on this subject, "it should be permissible for the parents not to be required to have the "A stamp." He points out that both England and Scandinavia have tried the mandatory requirement of normal hips for both parents and found that when too much emphasis was placed on one trait as a pre-condition to enter the show, it was at the expense of other breed traits.

Responsible breeders screen for possible eye conditions, as well as hip problems, before including that dog in a breeding program.

In Germany, the term "near normal" means a variation of the norm. In the United States, the term "near normal" means close, but not normal. The "best breeders" in Germany only breed the dogs that have an "A" stamp with a hip diagnosis of normal.

Breeding and Other Rules in Germany

The minimum breeding age allowed for sires is two years of age and for bitches 20 months (with some flexibility allowed depending on when they come into their first season).

Stud dogs are limited to 60 stud services each year. If more litters are born, those over 60 are not registered. These requirements serve to control over-usage, and it gives breeders more time to see what effect a stud dog has on the breed before his popularity affects the breed. This is just the opposite in the United States where a futurity system is used to identify promising young males before it is known what traits, diseases, or defects they will pass on to future generations.

Most German and European pedigrees include dogs from Belgium, Holland and Austria. The influence of these other blood lines is used to help make breed improvements.

Show Differences

There are differences in the rules of the show ring between the European, German and AKC systems. This table shows by comparison the key differences.

NOTE: SchH work involves three categories of work (tracking, obedience, and, cour-

CATEGORY	EUROPE (GERMANY)	AMERICA (GSDCA)
Utility Conf. Class	Must be 2 years of age	No such conformation class
Open Class	Not a conformation class	Any age to enter
Selects	Only at Seiger Show Must have SCH II * Must have "A stamp"	Only at National Show No working requirement No requirement for hips
Champion	No such title	AKC title
Temp Test in Ring	Judge establishes eye contact/approaches the dog	Judge establishes eye contact/approaches the dog
Info available to to judge in the ring	Pedigree, HD diagnosis, show and trail ratings (v,sg, g)	No information provided None allowed
Evaluations by judge	Conformation at 12 mos., first SchH I at 18 mos.	None by AKC or GSDCA
Rings at National	8, classes not staggered	2, classes staggered
Length of National	3 days, Fri., Sat., Sun.	3 days, Thur., Fri., Sat.
Regions	20	9
Clubs	1500	123
Members	100,000	4,000

*Must have SchH II and the following year SchH III, be surveyed, "A stamp" and complete dentition.

age). The differences between I, II and III are the levels of difficulty. Each level requires that the dog earn a minimum of 70 points. Each event allows the competitor to score up to 100 points for each test, with 300 points being a perfect score. All three categories must be passed to receive a working degree (SchH I, SchH II). The highest level (SchH III) requires a minimum score of 70 points for A and B, and 80 points for C.

Conformation showing is based on the dog's appearance—that is his structure, attitude and movement. This is Am.Can. Ch. Perracca's Mike winning at an outdoor show.

A local breeder is an excellent source for obtaining a German Shepherd puppy or an older dog.

Imports Versus American-Bred

The question of whether to buy an import or one from a local breeder is more complicated than it appears. There is nothing about being an import as opposed to one owned by a local breeder that makes them innately better. Perhaps the better question should be...What kind of dog is needed and for what purpose? If you only want a companion for your family and children, either will do, and the matter is one of cost. If you want one for herding, perhaps

The handsome and hearty appearance of the German Shepherd Dog has made him the choice of countless dog owners around the world.

the import might have the edge since many German-bred dogs are selected and trained for that purpose. Let's remember that many are not, so for those who want a herding dog, you should be sure and buy one from a breeder who selects his stock based on performance and who actively herds with the ones he bred.

I think that perhaps a better question about whether to buy and import or not might be based on the area where the gene pool has numerically large populations...Germany, United States, England, etc. In these countries there are many good stud dogs with outstanding pedigrees.

Importing dogs into the United States was popular until the 1970s. Thereafter, a slow decline occurred. It is difficult to know if it was a result of articles on the dangers of German imports (which some believed was nothing more than anti-German prejudice), or whether so many of the imports were of poor quality.

In 1993, this author had a meeting with Hermann Martin, president of the WUSV. He offered an interesting story about why imports are not sold to the United States. He reminded me that in 1992, at the World Trials (WUSV) held in Lintz, Austria, the highest ranked or the best German Shepherd Dog that year was purchased by someone from Japan. At the next year's trial the same dog with its Japanese owner returned to the competition and was ranked third. The question he posed to me was this, "Why would a breeder of a good dog sell it to an American when he knows that Americans do not bring their imports back for further competition, nor the offspring of the imports?" He concluded that a good

The German Shepherd Dog varies in color, and most colors are permissible. Here is an example of a solid black German Shepherd.

breeder would know that selling a good dog to an American means that it will be gone forever, and the breeder's reputation would not be enhanced by such a sale. He closed by saying, "That's why the better dogs are not sold to the Americans." He makes a good point even though some Americans have purchased quality imports and have brought them to World Competition. But overall his statement is generally true.

Imports are not cheap when you take into consideration the cost of transportation, insurance, and price of the dog. One cannot be impressed by the cost of a young import because it represents nothing more than someone who has the money to spend on a young dog. It provides no guarantees about quality or longevity. Imports should be selectively used and chosen with care. Their use should be to improve certain traits. They will not improve all of the traits because of the differences in the gene pools. The best use that has been made of imports has been to widely use them and inbreed them in order to concentrate on their gene pool. Their best daughters and granddaughters should be bred back to them or to their best sons. This concentrates the genes based on the sire's bloodlines rather than those of the dam's.

The practice of inbreeding in order to

concentrate on traits has produced excellent results in all breeds. In the German Shepherd breed one can easily recall the success that was achieved with Lloyd Brackett who produced over 100 champions. Inbreedings to Pfeffer v Bern and his offspring

Two German Shepherds are better than one! A lovely black and a black and tan enjoying the fresh country air.

influenced generations long after his death. Then there was the great import Troll v Richterback, whose type and success in the show ring is history. Although he produced many good qualities, he did produce large-sized offspring. It is difficult to know if the tendency to produce faulty front assemblies occurred because of his genetic make-up or whether it was the result of many poor quality bitches bred to him.

A beautiful black and tan German Shepherd Dog photographed by Karen Taylor.

SELECTING YOUR GERMAN SHEPHERD

PICKING THE RIGHT PUP

Buying a puppy should not be an impulsive endeavor. It is never wise to rush out and buy just any puppy that catches your shopping eye. The more time and thought you invest, the greater your satisfaction with your new companion. And if this new companion is to be purely a pet, its background and early care will affect its future health and good temperament. It is always essential that you choose a properly raised puppy from healthy, well-bred stock.

You must seek out an active, sturdy puppy with bright eyes and an intelligent expression. If the puppy is friendly, that's a major plus. You don't want one that is hyperactive nor do you want one that is dull and listless. The coat should be clean and plush, with no signs of fleas or other parasites. The premises of the breeder should be clean by sight and smell, and the proprietors should be helpful and knowledgable. A reputable seller wants his customers satisfied and will therefore represent the puppy fairly. Let good common sense guide your purchase, and choose a reliable, well-recommended source that you know has well-satisfied customers. Don't look for a bargain, since you may end up paying many times over in future veterinarian bills, not to mention disappointment and heartache if your pet turns out not to be temperamentally sound and healthy.

SELECTING A PUPPY TO SHOW

A puppy might grow up to be a good pet or he can be much more than that a blue-ribbon winner, a helpmate, a marvel of ability and certainly, a beloved companion. The pup's possibilities are restricted only by the owner's goals for him and by the selection process used to find this future Super Dog.

Choosing to share our lives with a dog is only the first step. We must determine also which breed best suits us and our lifestyle. It's wise to be prepared for several questions that will arise: Male or female? Adult or puppy? Did we select this breed for its special qualities and abilities or simply because we like its appearance or temperament?

Within a breed—even within a litter—per-

Choosing to share our lives with a dog is only the beginning of the dog-owner relationship. This is Epic's Color Me Bad of Zorago, "Marlo," at five weeks, owned by Gina Ostroman and Cathy Mekula.

Pups within the same litter will demonstrate various personalities. Choose the puppy who best suits your lifestyle; a shy pup would not be suitable for an active, outgoing individual.

whether competition in obedience or achieving a championship is a priority.

MAKING CONNECTIONS

When a serious fancier chooses a dog to fulfill hopes and dreams, more is involved than simply finding a litter of the chosen breed and picking the pup with the waggiest tail or the lickingest tongue. First, a breeder with an impeccable reputation must be found. For those who are already involved in the dog world, it's less difficult to make connections because they are aware of preferences in structure or in ability and have an idea as to which lines produce well in these respects.

sonality differences are found, and buyers should specify whether they want the one who bounces off the walls or the one who sleeps 23 hours a day. Other preferences, such as size or color, might be stated. A potential exhibitor should decide

The recent enthusiast may have to overcome a few more obstacles, but the goal is worth the trouble. When people want the best, they haunt the places where the best are found. When Cape Cod tourists crave a fresh clam bake, they go to the beach, not the all-night grocery. The finest wines are found at first-class restaurants, not at a lunch counter. And the same is true of dogs. According to various interests, the superior

When you are looking for the ideal pup, visit several breeders until you are satisfied that you have found the perfect match.

dogs will be at shows, trials or at test sites.

While studying the dogs who are esthetically pleasing and who perform in the manner admired, make notes about the kennels that boast about producing winners. Notice which sires and dams produce consistently. These are the owners to be considered as the blue-ribbon breeders. Even if these kennels do not have puppies available, they are the best places to start. Most owners are willing and able to recommend other breeders. Ask

Winning in the show ring requires a good dog that is well cared for as well as properly handled and conditioned. Gran Victor Polo is well proportioned and sturdy.

Breeders of champion dogs are the people to contact to begin your puppy search. Even if they have no available pups, they can recommend you to other good breeders who might. This fine litter was bred by Karin and Al Wagner.

these people if they can refer you only to places that they would buy from themselves. Giving a poor reference reflects on their own reputation; therefore, they stick to those with a four-star rating.

Starting at the root with a quality breeder allows a buyer to branch off if necessary. Show kennels have a monetary as well as an emotional investment at stake and seek excellence in the handlers, groomers and veterinarians with whom they do business. These professionals are additional sources of referrals. They often know who has litters, as well as who has top-notch animals and a

Dog clubs can put you in contact with breeders and other reliable contacts to locate your German Shepherd puppy.

squeaky clean reputation. Handlers, vets and groomers have a stake in the matter, too, because they might gain a client from someone who follows their lead and is pleased.

Dog clubs can supply reliable contacts as well. Many have a breeder index or an-swering services for just this purpose. The American Kennel Club can furnish the secretaries' names of sanctioned all-breed and specialty clubs, both locally and nationally. Often clubs are listed with the Chamber of Commerce or in the telephone book. The Kennel Club of Great Britain is the appropriate source for British residents, as is the Canadian Kennel Club for Canadians.

Some clubs have a code of ethics which the breeders must sign and adhere to in order to be recommended. Money-minded profiteers are seldom found within the ranks of clubs because they have no interest in supporting and working at shows, seminars or canine charity fundraisers.

Ads in canine magazines and newspapers are costly, and kennels who advertise are usually secure, well-established businesses with owners who have a reputation to maintain. It is up to us to determine just how fine that reputation is. "Brag" ads trumpeting the kennel's latest Field Trial Champion or Best in Show Winner can give clues of success within a specific field of interest.

Farah Von Nordrstein, owned by Ruth Zieleniewski, with two of her puppies.

Published breed books, such as this one, display photos of top-winning dogs and descriptions of the kennels that produced them. The motto, "Records live, opinions die" is a truism. Any kennel that claims winners numbering in the double digits or above has begun its own records.

Of course, the professional breeder who is just starting up the ladder offers advantages as well. Because he doesn't have the widespread reputation, he is less likely to have waiting lists. Frequently, the person from whom he bought his bitch or who owns the stud he used will refer inquiries to him.

Although cost should not be number one on our list when searching for a companion, it is a consideration for most of us, and a beginner seldom can demand the prices of the established breeder. If the dedicated newcomer has bought his foundation stock from a reputable kennel, very likely he will have animals for sale that are comparable in quality to his mentor's. Not everyone who looks for a new, snazzy car can afford to buy a Mercedes. Some of us have to be satisfied with a well-built Chevrolet. And that Chevy can be attractive and dependable too. We don't always

Clubs and local breeders can put you in contact with others who have dogs of a specific line or type. This is a nine-week-old puppy owned by Kaven Kierst.

have to buy top-of-the-line to obtain quality, as long as we stay away from the junkyard.

NETWORKING

In conducting any type of research, one lead suggests another. A contact list mushrooms and grows, giving the buyer several options.

When contacting a well-known kennel and finding no puppies available, it is helpful to ask, "Can you recommend someone?" Or, "I just love your stud, Alf (or your bitch, Tigger). Does anyone have puppies with those lines?" Who can resist a compliment like that?

Ask breeders whether they belong to a local club and the national breed club. Club membership shows a sustained interest in the breed and in dogs.

SEARCHING FOR SUPER DOG

Finding the ideal dog is not a whit easier than looking for the ideal mate. Of course, it's a bit less complicated to rid ourselves of an unwanted beast if it's the four-legged kind, but failure is not the object of conducting this search. It's finding a buddy, a companion, one who appeals to us in every sense and will still do so when he's old, gray and pot-bellied.

When it comes to welcoming a new member into a family, spending the time to find the right addition is well worth the effort. It can't be done by placing an ad in the personal want ad section: Tall, athletic man of 40 desires a jogging companion who is cute, fuzzy and has floppy ears.

How then? Buyers should look at several

Besides researching the breed, you should shop around and find the dog that best suits our lifestyle before you acquire your new German Shepherd pup. This is four-day-old Epic's Color Me Bad of Zorago, "Marlo," owned by Cathy Mekula.

Be sure you view a number of dogs before you decide on your pet. Puppies should not leave home before seven weeks of age.

examples of the breed before plunging into a ten-to-fifteen-year commitment. Many who have experience and have developed an "eye" know immediately whether or not a particular litter is going to offer promise. But those who are buying a dog for the first time or who are engaged in an initial search for this particular breed need to see more than one specimen to make such a decision. And it's best not to base a choice on a picture in a book or a television commercial, unless you've had the opportunity to see the dog in reality and in action.

Certain questions arise that can only be answered through a

The whole family, including small children, should be involved in the selection of your new German Shepherd puppy.

one-on-one session. Can I live with the energy of this breed/ individual? Is this dog too aloof for me?

Even if the dog of our dreams lives 2,000 miles away and it's impossible to make a speculative jaunt, buyers can observe the breed at shows or by hunting down a speci-

men that lives within 200 miles. Two hundred miles is too far? How far should you travel to find someone who is going to inhabit a corner of your life, your home and your heart for the next dozen years?

When the selection is narrowed down to one or two breeders and litters, and it comes to making a choice of the individual, this can be done even if the 2,000-mile trek isn't feasible. Of course, we have already ascertained that the breeder is reputable, so relying on his expertise and experience with the lines is helpful. Match-making is his business. He has everything to gain by ensuring the happi-

When selecting a puppy make sure the environment in which the pup is kept is clean and free of unpleasant odors.

ness of the new owner (and thereby the pup's) and everything to lose if it turns out to be a match made in hell.

Photos are a necessity in making a long-distance selection. Some modern-technology breeders offer videos to prospective buyers, demonstrating each puppy's movement, structure, attitude and interaction with littermates. A few think to film the sire during the nuptial visit and the dam prior to the loss of her willowy figure.

Professional handlers can assist in the search in return for a finder's fee and the promise of a new client. If the pro appears at the door with a scraggly hag instead of the voluptuous vamp of our dreams, it's no go and no dough.

ONE ON ONE

If we're fortunate enough to live in the same vicinity as the kennel, we can conduct our own evaluation and perhaps participate in a temperament or aptitude test of the litter. Certain other subtleties can be assessed as well, such as the breeder's rapport with his dogs. An unspoken but obvious bond should be present, passing from one to the other. . . a look of devotion when the dam looks at her owner. . . pride shining on the face of the breeder and soft affection for the dogs in his eyes. . . an almost automatic caress of a velvet ear during the buyer's interview. . . a wet nose nuzzling under an arm.

Happy, healthy dogs greet visitors at the door. Firm but gentle corrections are given and obeyed—at least partially, during the excitement of having guests. Needless to say, the sire and dam must be sound in mind and body as well as typical of the breed—that is, they look like Beagles instead of Bassets or vice versa. Although the sire is seldom a roommate of the dam, the breeder should have photos and pedigree of the dog available for viewing.

Buyers should be prepared to ask questions as well as to answer them. Does the breeder belong to a club, has he ever shown, and do any of his dogs have titles?

It is a good idea, if possible, to see the dam of the puppy that you intend to purchase. This handsome litter was bred by Al and Karin Wagner.

A good breeder should have answers to questions pertaining to the pup of your choice. He will also know about your dog's particular lineage and be sure of his good health.

Does he linebreed, inbreed or outcross? Negative answers do not necessarily mean "Buyer Beware." The breeder should have answers, however, to educated questions and not say, "Huh?" or "Got no time for such foolishness."

It is our duty to discover whether the breeder has taken steps to avoid hip and elbow problems. For instance, are his breeding animals OFA certified for good hips and good elbows. In addition to these hereditary conditions have the ancestors in the pedigree been checked? If we're interested in becoming breeders ourselves, a free-whelping line and superlative foundation stock are pluses. Free-whelping means the dam was an easy whelper, who showed much interest in her pups and had sufficient amounts of milk to support her litter. These traits are passed down from mother to daughter.

When appropriate, ask about and examine

for problems with, earsets, incorrect bites and missing teeth. If we've done our homework, faulty coats and colors should be apparent, but one should be aware of less obvious breed faults also.

MAKING THE GRADE

Those who wish to conduct formal temperament tests should do so when the puppies are seven weeks of age. These tests not only help breeders and buyers determine which pups are over-aggressive or horribly shy (hopefully none), but they show the range of good temperaments and obedience aptitude.

Pups should be tested separately, preferably on new turf by someone unknown to them. When the tester or surroundings is familiar, tendencies may be hidden or exaggerated.

In each instance, note whether the pups are bold, shy or curious. If a pup startles or is hesitant, does he recover and respond to the tester positively?

Temperament tests are designed to determine which pups are overly aggressive or shy. Pups should be tested separately and by someone unknown to them to obtain true results.

Social tests:

1. Observe the pup's reaction to the strange place and to a stranger. Is he bold, shy or curious? Note whether he bounces around immediately confident, hides in a corner or takes a moment to gain his composure and then begins to explore.

2. The tester should bend or kneel and call the puppy to him in a friendly manner, clapping or whistling if he wishes.

3. The tester should then stand and walk away, calling to the pup. Does he follow, run away or seem confused and immobile?

Dominance tests:

4. Rolling the pup on his back, the tester holds him in place for 30 seconds.

5. A stranger pets the pup on his head and looks directly at him, putting his face close to the pup's.

6. Pick up the pup with hands under the belly; hold elevated for 30 seconds.

Alertness/obedience tests:

7. Crumple noisy paper or rattle a stone inside a can.

8. Toss the paper or a toy to see if the pup retrieves and returns the object.

9. Drag a towel or similar object in front of the pup. Does he show curiosity and follow?

Responses:

The bold, naughty or aggressive pup reacts immediately, sometimes barking or biting. This pup struggles during the restraint or domi-

Socializing puppies with humans is essential in order to rear people friendly approachable dogs.

nance tests. He might grab at the tester's clothing. A top dog such as this one needs a dominant owner, a person who is willing—and able—to train, discipline and maintain control.

At the other end of the scale is the pup who shrinks away, shows disinterest or hides. He might cry or give in immediately during the restraint and dominance tests. The underdog takes a patient owner, one who is willing to encourage and socialize.

In between is the pup who is friendly, accepting and rather middle

Watching the way littermates interact with each other will give you a firsthand indication about the personality of the pup you are considering.

of the road. He might be hesitant, but is cooperative in most efforts. This one should fit in almost any home!

The ideal obedience prospect would willingly follow and come. He'd also be alert and show curiosity; he'd run after the toy, pick it up and return it to the tester.

NARROWING IT DOWN

Breeders have the additional advantage of living with the litter for eight or more weeks. They are the best ones to know which pup is the pack leader, which one follows docilely and which one tries to topple the king of the mountain off his perch. Notes should be made on eager or picky eaters. Individual descriptions

No one knows a pup's personality better than the breeder. When you have narrowed your choice down to two or three pups, ask for his/her advice.

using such adjectives as rowdy or laid-back, outgoing or aloof, and independent or willing to please are helpful during matchmaking.

When initial contact is made with the seller, we should specify what type of personality is desired in our future pet. A "type A" perfec-

Sometimes a pup will choose his owner before the owner chooses him. This pup has made his decision and will not let go!

tionist or workaholic will find it difficult to live with a rough-and-tumble, devil-may-care livewire who is trying out for the next *Rambo* sequel. Nor would the 78-year-old gent who likes to snooze by the evening fire want to go home with the canine yo-yo. (But this pup would be perfect for the athletic man wanting a jogging companion in that personal ad.)

The one absolute no-no is picking a dog because you feel sorry for him. Sorry lasts a long time. Rarely does a new home cure timidity, illness or anti-social behavior.

An owner who intends to exhibit his dog at shows or to

compete at obedience or agility trials wants to find one who has a good structure and high energy. Marked timidity shown during household pan rattling or door slamming wouldn't fare well for a dog who's expected to compete at these events. A bold, independent dog who shows curiosity is more desirable.

SELECTING THE FLYER

Those of us who have visions of red, white and blue Best in Show rosettes dancing in our heads look at type, structure, movement, and a certain indefinable quality

Before choosing a dog intended for show, know the breed standard and what a good specimen looks like. Show pups should not be selected before 8 weeks of age.

called presence. The best way to do this is to view the pups two or three at a time, ideally in a place which allows free movement and play: a fenced yard or a large room.

Any pup who exhibits disqualifying or serious faults should be eliminated from choice and from the examination site immediately. We can't take the chance of a sweet face turning us from our goal. Dogs of every breed who are blind or deaf, display viciousness or cryptorchidism (undescended testicles) as well as those that are neutered are specifically disqualified from conformation competition. Most breeds have additional disqualifications or serious faults—for example, size, color, coat or bite—and potential show buyers must be aware of these.

While the puppies are playing, look for the strut of canine royalty. Some dogs are born to show and they know it. They exhibit the panache of Clark Gable as Rhett Butler or sparkle like opening night at the opera. Given the choice, the ring-wise will opt for the pup with a less elegant neck and more charisma than for a deadhead swan.

Buyers should use the breed standard as a blueprint and study the pups, using heads and eyes rather than hearts. First on the list is a "typey" litter, fol-

German Shepherd Dogs are popular show dogs and there are often many in every class. Earning a championship can be very challenging.

lowed by the pup that is most representative. Pretend Great Aunt Minnie has seen only a picture of this breed. Which one could she look at and say, "Ah ha, *this* is a ...." Ideally, this pup will also possess the other physical requirements and have the spirit that makes him or her a special dog.

While examining bone, topline, shoulder and rear angulation, breadth and depth of chest, and length of body, a person should compare this to the blueprint standard in mind. Feel coat quality, taking into consideration the puppy coat. Is it fine or dense as required? Harsh or silky? The color, of course, should be acceptable. There is no sense in battling upstream with such an obvious fault which is so easily eliminated from selection.

Although personalities differ in dogs,

Your German Shepherd puppy may be cute curled up on your lap, but realize that he will not always be a "lap dog." Your cute little pup will grow into a dog between 24 and 26 inches.

sometimes with a wide normal range, temperament should be typical of the breed. No one buys a Chihuahua to guard their property, and probably few expect a Mastiff to curl up in their laps beyond infancy. The pup who displays confidence is always a better choice than one who cringes and shrinks from human touch.

Even if the standard calls for aloofness, puppies are usually blessed with an innocent sweetness. This characteristic makes them a delight to their family even if they grow to adulthood and snub everyone else. Whether the affection is demonstrated by a glow in the eyes, a single thump of the tail or bounding ecstasy at our approach, our dogs should like us . . . even if they don't like anyone else on earth.

Puppies *bounce,* puppies *boinnng,* puppies *galumph.* But, given enough time, the one who is put together in the proper way will demonstrate a baby version of exciting adult movement. We must be prepared to catch a glimpse into the future.

Many breeders produce dogs of a style and type that are highly desirable and therefore have long waiting lists. If you want a dog from such a breeder, your patience and investment will pay off.

BUYING A PIECE OF THE FUTURE

Some buyers place a deposit for a puppy sight unseen, sometimes even before the litter is born or bred! When we find a breeder who is producing the style, type and movement we want, it might be necessary to make a reservation long before our future dream pup sets paw on the ground. After all, if we admire what is trotting out of this kennel's gates, we should realize a few others might have recognized its quality as well. Breeders who consistently produce well often have long waiting lists.

Your newly purchased pup should come with a number of papers—a pedigree, a registration blank, medical records, feeding and grooming instructions, a sales contract and some type of health guarantee.

Before selecting a kennel to honor with the purchase, other factors can be discussed with the seller in advance. Be aware of the guarantee offered, what the contract covers and whether this kennel has established a reputation for standing behind its dogs.

Certain minimal records should accompany every pup: a pedigree, a registration blank, medical records, feeding and grooming instructions, a sales contract and some type of guarantee.

Registration papers are a necessity for the serious fancier who wishes to show and breed. Some dogs that can not be registered as pure bred dogs can be given an ILP (Individual Listing Privilege) number and may be shown in obedience with a Limited Registration. These dogs may also participate in a few instinct tests, but may not be exhibited in the conformation ring. The American Kennel Club requires ILP dogs (other than those in the Miscellaneous Classes) to be spayed or neutered, and the Limited Registration stamp, begun in 1990, prevents the limited dog's progeny from being registered. These steps were taken by the AKC to discourage indiscriminate breeding practices.

A pedigree should contain at least three generations, with four to six being preferable. Pedigrees tell us more than the names and titles of ancestors. The knowledgeable dog person can see whether a pup is

Although white German Shepherd Dogs have many adoring fans, none of them will be found in the AKC show ring, as white is a disqualification according to the breed standard.

linebred, outcrossed or inbred. Health certifications also are added such as OFA and CERF numbers. Many of the newer pedigrees will include coat length and colors. A pedigree strong in obedience titles should give an indication that the pup's family demonstrates trainability and intelligence. Likewise, several championship

Your puppy's vaccination schedule should begin at six to eight weeks of age and continue until 14 to 16 weeks.

titles are encouraging. Quality begets quality.

An eight-week-old pup should not have a lengthy medical record, but this paper should note a physical exam and at least one combination inoculation. If the litter has been wormed, this should also be noted.

A good age to pick a puppy is when the litter is from eight to ten weeks old. By this time, they have learned canine socialization skills from their dam and littermates. With plenty of TLC given by the breeder as a background, sound puppies easily transfer their affection to a new family.

Lines and breeds vary, but many knowledgeable breeders

prefer to pick their show prospects between eight to twelve weeks of age. Follow the breeder's advice; nobody knows the lines better than he does.

Occasionally the subject of co-ownership arises. This may create the best of times or the worst of times; it certainly forges the members of a paper relationship into the best of friends or festers them into the worst of enemies. An offer of co-ownership does signify that the breeder has faith in the dog. After all, he wouldn't want to co-own a poor specimen.

A decision can be made depending upon the strings of the co-ownership and whether the two parties can

If you do your homework, you will be successful in picking a fine German Shepherd pup that will grow into the dog you have always dreamed of!

work together. Simple co-ownership agreements may require one puppy back from a breeding or stud rights. More complicated contracts demand half a litter— or half of every litter, exhibition requirements, hiring an expensive professional handler, or more. If breeder and buyer are congenial and willing to bend when situations not covered in the contract arise, a co-ownership can be an opportunity to purchase a dog or bitch that normally would be beyond one's price range.

PAPER WORK

Sales contracts should cover the information listed on the registration blank, so that there is no misunderstandings about who the pup is or its parents.

A good contract should include a short period of time until the buyer can take the puppy to a veterinarian. If there is a problem at that time, a full refund should be given. Most reputable buyers also give a health guarantee covering various con-genital defects which arise by the age of one year—one year, because most have appeared by that time; congenital, because the seller cannot be expected to cover injuries or illnesses. Should a congenital defect appear after this age, some contracts call for replacement of the pup only if it has crip-pling hip dysplasia as certified by a vet; others specify that if the pup fails to OFA at two years of age, the seller would be willing to discuss a replacement.

Show puppy contracts usually cover serious and disqualifying faults as stipulated in the breed standard. All contracts and guarantees should be read carefully by the buyer. If any clauses are objectionable or questionable, ask for an explanation before signing.

Although the pup won't come with an operator's manual that directs you to "Put tab A into slot A" or have a bag attached with extra nuts and bolts, instructions should be part of the package. This will cover suggested puppy diet, feeding schedule, housebreaking suggestions, and grooming particulars. Written advice on crates, training classes, and recommended reading material may have more than one use. It helps fill the wee morning hours when the pup misses his warm, fuzzy siblings and wails his loss to the world.

When you first bring home your new pup, he may become lonely for his littermates. Give him some time and space to adjust—he'll soon bond to you as his surrogate mom and brethren.

At 15 weeks this German Shepherd has a lot of growing to do. It is a nice idea to send the dog's breeder a photo or letter about the dog's latest accomplishments. Good breeders never want to lose touch with the dogs they have raised.

The purchase is only the beginning of a long relationship between buyer and seller. There are questions to be answered, pleasant stories to be shared and fears to be calmed. Photos of the little guy opening his Christmas presents, bathtime, the teenage uglies, entering his first puppy match and finishing his championship are treasured keepsakes for the breeder.

Sounds complicated, but puppies have an advantage over most purchases with moving parts. They come ready to use, all wound up and ready for action— no batteries needed. Nor is it necessary to plug in the pup to make him wag his tail or wash your face. In case of power failure, we don't even miss the electric blanket.

BENEFITS OF OWNERSHIP

The benefits of owning a German Shepherd are many... among them pride, responsibility and social acceptance. We are often proud of owning a beautiful animal (remembering that beauty is in the eye of the beholder) whose coat shines with health and whose eyes sparkle with glee at our approach. We can make friends and establish relationships through our dog. Kids and adults both learn responsibility through caring for the pet. We educate ourselves to provide physical care and, if we so desire, the intricacies of the dog world—as far as we want to go. Our dog doesn't care at what stage we stop learning. Acceptance comes because our dog al-

The bond that grows between an owner and his German Shepherd is strong and everlasting.

ways greets us with affection, no matter what our age, race, creed, size or abilities.

But probably the most important benefit is psychological. No matter what happens in our day-to-day life, there is always someone who cares, someone who asks little in return. Our dog provides us with a reason to rise in the morning, a reason to exercise, a reason to prepare food and, in some cases, a reason to live. We're never alone when we're in the company of a good friend.

With the proper training and kindness, your new German Shepherd puppy will give you a lifetime of happiness.

Coat and Color

The main pigment of the mammal is melanin of which there are two basic forms: eumelanin (brown or black) and phaeomilanin (yellow or reddish). The color of a dog's coat is dependent on the presence or absence of these melanin types in the cortex and medulla of the hair. Since most breed standards state that color is one aspect of evolution there is no justification for judges who award ribbons and points to inferior animals of their own favorite color in preference to superior animals of light tan, black, or bicolors.

The basic colors of the breed can be divided into four broad categories:

Sables: This is the dominant color of the breed and may vary in shade from grey to intense gold.

Black-and-tan: The black varies from a saddle to covering a larger area of the body down to the pasterns, but not the eyes and chest. The tan can also vary in shades from a rich red or gold through a pale fawn or even light cream.

Black: The entire body, feet, tail, and head are black with no other color present.

Black is one of the four recessive colors in the breed; the other three are blue, liver and white.

White: These dogs vary somewhat from a clear bright white through a dirty yellow white.

All of these basic colors are acceptable except those that are pale or washed out, and whites which are disqualified. Blues do occur but they appear to be sable or black-and-tan and might be grouped into this shade, though caused by other factors.

There is no evidence of sex linkage in color in the breed. But the color of the German Shepherd Dog is more complex in its inherit-ance than one might suspect because there are many shades of tan and variable patterns, which cause confusion about how to code color at the time of registration. The color of the coat is also controlled by a pair of genes. While there are many shades of color in the breed

Moonshadow Sunset Serenade, a white German Shepherd Dog owned by Licia Babb.

the transmission of each shade including the patterns, intensity, and density of pigments are complex and generally not well understood. Unfortunately, little research has been conducted on the genetics of color

The length of the coat is controlled by genes. In a litter of pups, there may be only one pup that has a long coat, however, this means that both parents are carriers of the long-coat factor.

and there is no agreement about color terminology or how color combinations are produced or interpreted. For example, the color called liver in the German Shepherd is called red in Doberman Pinchers and brown or chocolate in other breeds.

In the German Shepherd breed the dominant color is sable, followed by the black-and-tan, bicolor, agouti, black, blue, liver and white. Four of the colors are produced by a pair of recessive genes and will occur by mating two dogs together that each carry at least one recessive gene for the color produced. For example, the white pup can only occur if both

In order to produce a black dog, both parents must contribute a black gene to the genetic makeup. This 15-week-old black German Shepherd pup is owned by Kaven Kierst.

of its parents passed on one white gene to the offspring. This makes the parents a carrier of the white factor. The same principle holds true for dogs that are black, liver and blue. Agouti is the grey wolf-like color. Light or faded pigment in the German Shepherd Dog, such as light tan, is not popular among breeders and judges because the breed standard calls for "strong rich" colors of pigment.

White is disqualified by the standard because it fails to meet the pigment requirement, meaning that the coat should be deep and rich in pigment. Liver and blue are considered undesirable colors and are faults by the standard and in the show ring. Black is an acceptable color that is not faulted by the standard. It is also controlled by two recessive genes. In order to produce any one of the four recessive colors both parents must carry at least one of the recessive genes for the recessive color and then pass it onto their offspring. A black-and-tan sire bred to a black-and-tan dam could produce any one of the four recessive colors if they both were a carrier of the recessive color. In one litter they could produce a black, black-and-tan, liver and blue. When any of the recessive colors occur like that, the breeder knows that both parents were carriers of the recessive colors that were observed. It also suggests that if there were black-and-tan littermates they probably will be carriers of the recessive colors seen in their brothers and sisters.

Color breeding is a subject that usually gets the attention of all breeders. It is a subject that most would like to know more about. Unfortunately, it is not possible to write a definitive explanation that is conclusive given the many shades and patterns of color that can occur. The size of the mask on the face or the

Nine-week-old black and tan German Shepherd Dog owned by Ruth Zieleniewski.

Breeders are encouraged to keep accurate breeding records; this will ensure the information recorded in the stud book is correct. Darby Dan's Audi owned by Dan and Sandy Smith.

black saddle on the back are areas that have not been studied and there is only limited data on which to base certain conclusions. Besides the limited information, there is always the problem of the inaccurate recording of colors for the ances-tors shown in pedi-grees. Information about color comes from the AKC color codes which appear on the Registration Form. What is needed is a color chart which shows the colors in the breed. Because pups sometimes change from the color they are born with to a lighter or darker shade, the light tans, blacks, and reds, and even bicolors will change after they are registered. When this happens the data for the colors recorded in the stud book lose some of their accuracy. In the final analysis, breeders need to be encouraged to keep accurate records.

The reader of this chapter by now has already concluded that the subject of color is inevitably going to lead to some Mendelian theory of heredity. The laws of simple Mendelian inheritance hold that for certain characteristics the parents will transmit to their offspring genes in an orderly fashion. Certain factors may be dominant, others recessive; this may be explained by saying that a dominant factor is stronger than a recessive and when present it will be obvious as a character trait even though a recessive factor also is present in the genotype. For example, in color genetics, brindle is

White Shepherds are disqualified in the conformation ring but can be shown in obedience and herding trials.

dominant to white. In the language of the geneticist, capital letters are used to represent a dominant trait (B), and lower case letters to represent a recessive trait (b). To illustrate this point let B = brindle and b = white. A brindle animal may therefore be represented either as

The color of your German Shepherd Dog has no bearing on his personality or health. If not intended for show, the dog's color is truly a matter of personal preference.

Bb or BB. The brindle with the Bb composition shows the character of brindle since the brindle factor is dominant to white. The white animal must have the composition bb. If a brindle factor were present the brindle character would show up. But if two brindle animals were bred, the possibilities are as follows:

BB   X   Bb

BB BB Bb Bb

The dog represented as BB is known as homozygous (or pure) for the brindle and the Bb, as heterozygous (impure) and it will be seen from the above example.

Although brindle is not a color of the German Shepherd Dog, one can substitute the color

Rich dark pigment is desirable in all German Shepherd Dogs. Notice this puppy's particularly dark face and eyes.

sable for brindle or for other dominant colors and get the same results.

WHY A DISQUALIFICATION?

The color white is often associated with deafness but this appears to be only for those dogs that are produced from the M allele. The German Shepherd carries the mm allele but not the M allele, and thus it would be incorrect to deduct that deafness or blindness will come from white dogs. The early history of the breed shows that many of the outstanding sires of the breed have produced white pups. If one uses white dogs in their breeding program, they are likely to see increasing numbers of offspring with pale colors.

In the early days of the breed (late 1800s) when the herding and working aspects focused on the role of a protector from the wolf, many of the herding breeds were white so that they were less noticed from the sheep. Today, many of the large working breeds in Europe still demonstrate this color advantage to carry out their work. But the German Shepherd was never a herding dog that was preferred to be white. It was different in that it was a dog that was needed to be seen by the herder. Not a dog that was the same color as the sheep or the snow. A dark dog aided the herder, who could easily spot its location and command it to move the sheep. For this reason, white was a disadvantage and therefore not desired in the breed. In other areas in which the breed has been so well noted such as military, police and guard work, the white dog has generally been considered to be at a disadvantage because of its visibility at night. For guide work and as a companion, white is of little or no consequence. Most whites are culled at birth making those who survive a "rare" white. Some kennels have specialized in white or black but they usually include dogs of other colors in their breeding program in order to maintain many of the breed's desired working and conformation traits.

COAT

With few exceptions, most mammals have a coat of hair. In the canine species, there are generally two distinct types of coats; an undercoat (under hair) and an outer coat (over hair). The undercoat is composed of thin downy hairs and the outer coat of various hair types, which are the long, thick and usually straight hairs. These long hairs are also known as guard hairs.

The length of the coat is another trait that is

Some kennels specialize in breeding the white German Shepherd Dog but include colored dogs in their breeding program in order to maintain many of the breed's working and conformation traits.

controlled by a pair of genes. Again both parents must carry the coat factor for the long coat to appear in their offspring. In a litter of six pups, there might be only one pup with a long coat. When this one long coated pup occurs, it always signals that both parents are carriers of the long coat factor. It is also a good bet that its littemates, who have normal length coats, are carriers of the long coat gene. It should be remembered that in the canine species, the short length coat is always dominant over the long coat. The Breed Standard for the German Shepard Dog considers the long coat a fault but does not disqualify it from competition.

Long-coat three-month-old puppy. Notice the long hair around the edge of the ear and inside the ear.

Management

Many things are involved in the raising and caring for a German Shepherd Dog. The most popular factors include the environment, nutrition and training. These are the key ingredients that usually result in what makes a German Shepherd Dog's performance. The question of genetics, too, can not be ignored because behavior and performance are under the control of both. Genetics control at least 35% of the behavior, and the remaining 65% are under the influence of nutrition and management.

EXERCISE

Healthy pups like to play until they are tired. If left to themselves they will rest when they are tired, but when kept with people they will continue to play. So, what appears to be endless energy can be misleading.

Growing bodies need rest and exercise to grow properly. A puppy's body is not designed to keep pace with people, who can play for longer periods of time without rest. Pups do not have bodies that can keep up with older animals. Because they are growing, they are not yet

For a puppy, exercise can consist of a short walk around the yard. Don't overdo exercise with your young German Shepherd. This is Van Cleves Luke.

capable of keeping up with the older, more mature animals. If left together with the older dogs, they will over exercise their bodies causing injury to their soft joints. Many promising pups, with proper angulation and balance, end up as only average adults, lacking angulation with weak backs and unbalanced movement. Sometimes over-zealous owners exercise young dogs too much by throwing a ball for long periods of time or allowing it to fence-run for long periods with adults. The pup is willing because it has good play drive, but the body is not ready for such extended amounts of exercise. Controlling exercise until the pup is fully grown always gives the body a better chance to develop properly.

BATHING AND GROOMING

The best rule to use when you think about bathing your Shepherd is to remember that he only needs to be bathed when he is dirty or smelly. Bathing too often can remove natural oils making his coat and skin dry and itchy. When selecting a shampoo, only use one that is made for dogs, as the pH level of a pet's skin is different the pH used in shampoos for humans.

Brushing is another matter. For the best results, brush the dog once each day. If time does not allow, once every few days, but at least once a week. Brushing helps stimulate natural coat oils, prevents tangles and is a great way to check for external parasites, such as ticks and fleas. The best way to brush your Shepherd is to back brush the hair. Back brushing the coat means to brush it in the opposite direction from which it naturally

To avoid having your dog shed hair around the house, regular brushing is necessary.

grows. When brushing, be sure to brush under the stomach, the legs and tail. When finished, dampen a towel and back rub the coat. Leave it that way and allow the moisture from the towel to collect the dust. Cleaning the coat regularly this way will give it more body and it will have a healthy look and feel. The dampened coat will dry in a few minutes and the coat will return itself to its natural position.

Grooming should be a comfortable experience for your dog. This should not be too difficult if you accustom your dog to being handled as a puppy. Good grooming techniques include a warm and friendly voice and will also make han-

Grooming tools remove the dead hair from your German Shepherd's coat.

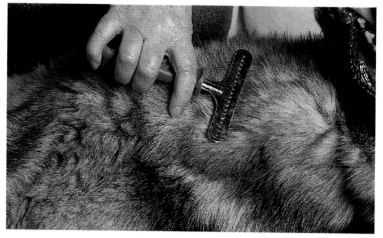

dling of the dog easier when it becomes an adult.

BRUSHING TEETH

One of the most popular ways to clean teeth is with a dog biscuit or a large beef bone. Both have some benefit, but neither prevent the buildup of plaque and tartar. This is why it is so important to brush the teeth regularly. Once a week with a tooth brush and a dog tooth paste will do the job.

HAND-SHYNESS

Hand-shyness is a condition that makes most dogs undesirable, because they avoid contact with humans. It generally becomes a deleterious problem for both the dog and owner because hand-

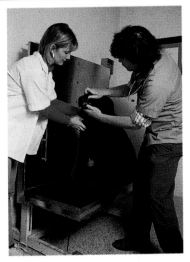

Veterinary examinations will be made easier if your German Shepherd Dog is used to being handled.

shyness is seen as a sign of discomfort. Dog show judges see it when the dog pulls away, and avoids being touched and refuses to stand for the required examination. During veterinary examinations dogs may resist handling and are unwilling to be treated,

Proper socialization begins at a young age with handling and interaction with humans as well as dogs.

cheating the owner of the best treatment available. The consequences of such behavior range from dog to dog, with some showing signs for aggressive behavior.

While pups are still in the nest, it is a good idea to begin touching them all over their bodies. Verbal assurances and praise help the process. Some of the more timid puppies may prefer to hide and avoid handling. They will need more attention and may become a problem to place with a suitable owner later. The sight of a favored treat or squeak toy are good aids when training and socializing pups.

Desensitizing exercises involve exposing the pup to whatever is frightening to it, including strangers and children. Training and socializing pups should never be punitive, particularly for those that are shy.

SHAPING BEHAVIOR

Most pups will respond to repetition and

positive reinforcement. There are only two ways to dominate behavior in the dog. One is to use force and the other is to dominate. Force is achieved several ways. While not recommended, these methods include verbal and physical abuse, shock collars and the misuse of training aids. The preferred method of eliciting the desired behavior in a dog is through dominance.

Dominance works best because it is understood by canines. It is accomplished by learning to rule over the dog in a just manner. The proper exertion of dominance is simply a form of guidance which is used to influence behavior. It works much like the way a pack leader establishes so-

In addition to learning hand and voice signals for commands, the dog must learn signals for corrections. This dog is being corrected to stay.

cial control over others. Dominance is a natural instinct of the canine and it is what social relationships are based on, especially between a pup and its mother, and a pup and its trainer. The misuse of dominance is the cruel use of power and interferes with most training situations. The best example of the misuse of dominance is the situation where nothing less than the absolute and immediate response is acceptable. Usually, in these situations the trainer is trying to show off to others or is angry that the dog does not respond as expected.

Every pup's personality is different and not all will learn at the same pace. Be patient with your training and set short-range and long-range goals for yourself and pup.

One of the best ways to get the desired results, when training, is to establish some long range objectives. The experienced trainer knows that all dogs will not be able to learn at the same rate and there will always be a situation in which the dog seems to resist learning.

Seeing the big picture in managing the career of a young pup is important for getting the desired results. Things go wrong for the pup and owner when time becomes the enemy and the goal becomes achieving quick results. Under these conditions trainers try to hammer a pup into the mold of another dog. Being rough and short tempered rarely accomplishes anything meaningful and does not mold them into the desired adult.

Reward is always the best training aid because it encourages good behavior, strengthens the dog/master bond and creates a happy and willing atmosphere. Under these conditions the link between

Dog trainer Max Lee training his dog to "play dead."

training and pleasure becomes possible.

Shaping behavior is accomplished by rewarding the activity that is desired. Rewards should be earned not given away. During each training session the trainer should be careful not to just give a pat on the head or a word of encourage-

Training your German Shepherd puppy can begin as early as eight weeks of age. Reward him when a desired action is completed.

ment if the pup has not earned it. If you do the pup is not sure what to do to get the reward. In a learning situation, if the dog learns that you will reward him with pats, kind words or treats all the time, he becomes confused and wonders what is the command and why do it. Rewards that are not earned only confuse the dog. As soon as the animal associates the desired behavior with the command, the condition for the correct response can occur.

Teach one thing at a time. One task at a

time should be the method of training. When something is being asked by the trainer, a reward should always be connected to the behavior. The first rule is that rewards are the only way to teach new behavior. The second rule involves punishment and its best use is to suppress undesirable behavior. Experience shows that rewards and punishment are both necessary if consistent and reliable behavior is expected.

The third rule is that punishment should only be intensive enough to be effective

Rewards should be given in all types of training, even when training your pup to go to a desired area outdoors for elimination.

Be consistent with your training methods and always praise your pup lavishly for proper behavior. Hugs and kisses can work just as well as food rewards.

when applied. It must be given immediately because it links punishment with the undesired behavior. Immediately means within 5—10 seconds. Sometimes during training/work the pup willingly carries out a command but it is the wrong response for what you wanted. For example, you may tell the pup to sit and it lies down instead. Don't punish and confuse the pup. Quickly review the training sequence and establish why the dog misunderstood the command. In this case, show the pup what you want and then reward it while saying, "good, sit." The fourth rule is to be consistent and predictable. Too often trainers reward certain behavior one day, punish it the next and ignore it on the third day. The scenario that I recall involves a trainer who calls his pup and it did not come. He called it repeatedly but the pup continued to do other things. In anger the pup is chased, caught and punished. What has the pup learned? From the pup's point of view, when he is called he will be chased and punished. What is he supposed to do? His best choice is not to respond to being called. On the second day, not remembering the punishment given the first, the owner calls the pup while it happens to be coming toward him, when the pup arrives he gets rewarded. What did he learn?...On the third day the trainer calls the pup who is in the yard, just then the phone rings and he leaves. Much later he returns and calls the pup again. What is the pup supposed to do this time? He has been confused by three different and inconsistent training commands and rewards.

GENERAL RULES OF TRAINING

Don't try to change the natural inclination of the pup. If you do, you may break his desire to try to learn and be trained.

Don't start too early and expect that he will want to learn everything that all the other dogs have learned.

Your puppy's full attention is needed during training sessions. Bring him to an area free of distractions for his lessons.

Remember he is a pup who has a lot of investigating to do before he is ready to learn.

Don't punish him for past mistakes. What happens today has nothing to do with what happened yesterday. He has already forgotten it. When training young dogs, getting them to do the command is more important than how well it is performed. When we as children first started to read, it was not that you had to get every word right, but more importantly that you were reading. Improvements come later with repetition and rewards.

Building confidence occurs when the pup always wins. The last activity should always be something that will result in a positive reward. Remember that confidence comes one step at a time, and usually it means that little things count. The fact that the pup will sit or chase the ball is what's important, not whether he picks it up and dashes back with perfection.

DOMINANCE EXERCISES

There are several handling techniques that can be used early in the life of a pup to help establish you as the dominant partner.

Begin when the pup is eight weeks old with the first excercise (evaluation). Start by lifting the pup up to your eye level holding it behind the front legs for a period of 30 seconds. Look directly into the pup's eyes. If it struggles, shake it gently and raise your voice. Praise it softly while it settles down. Repeat the exercise daily in different places so that the pup associates dominance in many places and in the presence of other people. Do this for three to five weeks.

The second exercise (inversion) is to hold the pup upside down

Caesar, CDT owned by Victoria M. Waite learning the down command.

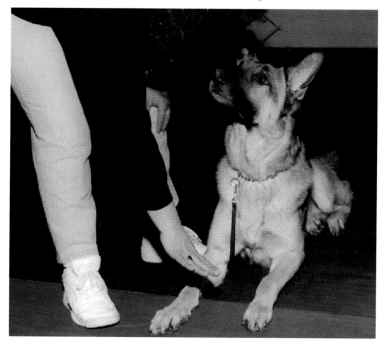

with one hand on the scruff of the neck and the other below its rump. Hold it away from you. If it struggles, shake it gently.

The third exercise (straddling) is to straddle the pup between your legs as if to ride it. Lock your hands under its chest just behind the front legs

The first objective in training is to have control over your dog. Dominance tests are used early in the life of a pup to help establish you as the dominant figure.

and lift the pup off the floor. If it struggles shake it and raise your voice.

The fourth exercise (lying prone) is to lay the pup on its side on the floor and hold it there using the same technique as in the other exercises. Touch all parts of its body including putting your fingers inside its mouth.

Remember...repeat these exercises in different places and within the presence of others.

In the training of your dog , the first objective is to gain control of the dog so that learning can be focused.

SELECTION OF MATES

In the breeding of German Shepherd Dogs, the question of potential partners

Planned matings help to obtain puppies of a specific type. Although the element of luck cannot be discounted, breeders are able to predict the likely results of a mating.

must be addressed with serious interest. The selection of mates involves many things. The first step is to compare the dogs against the breed standard. In some breeding programs the process and the decision to select sires and dams is founded on the belief that performance is inherited. Attempts to analyze the genetics of performance in a systematic way is not new. Distinguished names such as Charles Darwin and Francis Galton attempted to explain how genetics and selection favored the breeder. Today modern science has found ways to better predict some of the traits that are likely to occur in a litter when certain sires and dams are mated. The technique is called "estimates of heritability," which is useful for predicting the likelihood that certain traits of conformation might occur. The heritability estimate is another way to calculate, using mathematics, the traits that are likely to occur in the next generation. It is based on how closely ancestors and relatives resemble each other for various traits. For example, you would expect a group of half-siblings to have a greater degree of similarity than a group from non-related individuals. For example, litter size has low heritability, around 10-15%. This is because litter size is largely determined by non-additive factors of dominance. In genetic terms, heritability can be grouped into three categories: low (20% and below), medium (30-50%), and high (50% or more). Good managers, who utilize the power of heritability estimates, can improve certain traits in their

A white pup owned by Licia Babb. Although the white gene is a recessive gene, one white gene from each parent must be inherited in order for it to appear in the phenotype.

A trio of black and tan German Shepherd Dogs. Notice the family resemblance, from left to right: Epic's Command Performance (son), Epic's Feature Presentation (daughter), Ch. Cobert's Smokescreen (mom).

future litters by more carefully selecting sires and dams whose pedigrees show ancestors with the traits desired. Heritability estimates are typically expressed as a range of values such as 50% to 75%, the lower percentage is used for outcrossed dogs, while the higher percentage is used for line bred or inbred dogs.

It is not accidental that some breeders have been able to consistently produce certain traits more often than others. The following table is helpful in understanding why some traits can more easily be produced. Remember, the higher the heritability estimate for a trait, the more likely it will occur in the offspring. Traits with low heritability estimates are easily influenced by the environment. For example, if the height of the stud is 20 inches and the dam is 17 inches, their offspring should be somewhere between 17 and 20 inches.

Notice that the heritability estimates for short pasterns (50%) and wither height (40—65%) is higher than temperament (30—50%). Also, remember that it is more likely for a trait to occur in the offspring if both parents were

Only good-quality representatives of the breed should be used in a breeding program.

Pella Jimeni Friday Morning, owned by Elena Strangel and Jim Hall. Judge, Dr. Carmen Battaglia.

observed to have the traits or if both had produced them in other litters. Taking this one step further, a good breeding would be to use prospective parents whose littermates were also observed to have the traits desired.

For example, a sire that had four of his six littermates, with three desired traits, is a better candidate than another that only had one of six littermates with the same three desired traits. The same of course is true of the dam. It goes without saying that the more ancestors there are with the traits desired, the more likely they will occur in the offspring.

Feeding Your German Shepherd

This chapter explores a wide range of issues related to the German Shepherd Dog as it grows and develops and how it should be raised. It discusses changes in nutritional requirements with age and some of the more popular management practices that work.

There is not one way to feed dogs. Therefore, I have included several of the better ideas that work. The reader should enjoy the ideas on how to maintain good health, and the feeding of a complete and balanced diet. For those who think of nutrition and care as simply the feeding of a dry meal supplemented with table scraps and other tidbits, read on for some good information about commercial dry meals, and what owners of fast-growing dogs need to know.

NUTRITION

Your German Shepherd Dog is a carnivore, a flesh eater. Its teeth are fashioned for tearing and severing, not for grinding as are human teeth. Over many decades some have erroneously concluded that the dog must be fed mostly on muscle meat in order to properly develop.

Those who think that way usually refer to the wolves, jackals, wild dogs and foxes which are all relatives to your dog. Keep in mind that all of those listed stalk and run down their food. As predators they have as their main prey the various hoofed herbivorous animals, small mammals and birds of their native habitat. Carnivores consume the entire body of their prey, not just the muscle meat. Their manner of feeding has led some zoologists to consider the dog as omnivorous (plant and animal eater) despite their

Water is an essential element for all forms of life. Be certain to supply your dogs with plenty of fresh water especially if they are to be outdoors for long periods of time.

obvious relationship to the carnivores within their family.

As hunters they first lap the blood of their victim, then tear open the stomach and eat the contents which is composed of predigested vegetable matter. Next they eat the liver, heart, kidneys, lungs and the

Most dogs enjoy lapping water directly from the hose. Remember, your German Shepherd needs more water in the hot weather.

fat-encrusted intestines. The bones and the tasty marrow that they contain, are eaten last along with the lean muscle meat. To supply the same essentials to your Shepherd in a form that you can easily purchase, dog food manufacturers have developed a dry meal. Fortunately for breeders and owners, the competition for profits has forced dog food manufacturers to produce what has come to be known as the million dollar formula, or the nearly perfect dog foods. These new and advanced formulas are complete and do not need supplements because they are balanced products. Altering these quality

Stainless steel feeding bowls are the best for your dog as they are durable and easy to clean and sterilize.

feeds with supplements of calcium, vitamins, oils, cheese, eggs, etc., alters the million dollar formula and affects the growth and development of the pup.

The large and giant breeds, like the German Shepherd Dog, which grow rapidly, must be more carefully fed than the smaller and slower growing breeds. The measure of whether a dog food is of high quality is based on its contents, digestibility and palatability.

The German Shepherd Dog is one of the large breeds that is known to have an accelerated growth pattern. Supplementing pups that are being fed quality dry foods not only alters the manufacturer's formula but also alters the growth and health of the animal. I call it nutritional insult that oftentimes causes bones to grow in an irregular manner and tendons to collapse, especially in the front and rear legs.

For those who want to change the diet of their young pup, I offer a word of caution. A change in the diet of most dogs and pups will usually result in diarrhea or soft stools unless carefully managed. The digestive system of canines is designed for routine diets with little tolerance for variety.

Therefore, when a diet is changed, it should always be done gradually, usually over a seven to ten day period. Puppies whose stools are loose should be fed boiled white rice until the stools firm up. If results are not forthcoming in two or three days, consult a veterinarian.

WEIGHT

German Shepherd pups grow rapidly, which means they also need plenty of rest. Allowing them to become heavy and fat will cause them to have soft backs and barreled ribs when they become adults. It takes patience to grow a quality dog, much like the patience that parents invest in managing the development of their children. For those who have the time, three small meals each day are better than one large feeding.

By spreading the daily ration over three meals the owner is able to distribute the weight carried in the stomach that pulls down on the back. This may be subtle, but reducing the weight in the stomach in turn lessens the stress on the back of an active pup that is running and jumping. Not allowing the back to carry heavy stom-

After weaning, puppies should be fed a good puppy chow that is finely ground and mixed with warm water.

Nylafloss®, a nylon tug toy that acts like a dental floss, is great for puppies to play with as it will provide them with hours of entertainment.

ach loads during the growth period increases the chances that it will develop into a strong and firm top line as an adult. The problem of feeding once per day usually results in a very hungry pup, who at meal time wants to fill up and over eat. When finished they have a pot belly full of water and food.

Pups left together after nine weeks often learn to compete for food at feeding time, which in some cases causes them to over eat. This is one of the problems of feeding one large meal to the whole litter. The hunger of the larger pups usually causes them to bully the others and then to try and eat it all. These over-eaters will force their soft rib cages to follow the contour of their pot bellies. As they grow and develop, their soft ribs stiffen but instead of being slightly rounded, they harden into a bowed or barreled ribcage. Another problem related to these over eaters is that they gain too much weight too fast. The weight that they gain is carried in their stomachs which affects the development of their overall structure. The vertebrae of the back are soft and, like the cartilage of the rib cage and other joints of the body, are comprised mostly of soft material. As they grow and develop, the skeleton begins to stiffen into bone. During the accelerated growth period (nine weeks to nine months) these skeletal structures are at their greatest risk of being damaged. Since the backs and joints of puppies are not designed to withstand

For those hot summer days, your German Shepherd should always have a large bowl of fresh water available to drink, and to play with as well!

heavy weight and stretching, the serious owner needs to control weight and minimize exercise immediately after feeding. Once stretched or pulled out of their original shape, cartilage and soft body parts will never return to their original shape.

PUPPY NUTRITION

Basic Foods and Supplements

The necessary ingredients for dogs can be found in the grocery store. Manufacturers by law are required to list the essential dietary requirements on their products. The list includes several items. I have added to the list the most often used sources that are used to meet those requirements:

1. Protein: meat, dairy products, eggs, soybeans
2. Fat: butter, oil, cream, fatty meat, milk, cheese
3. Carbohydrates: cereals, vegetables, honey
4. Thiamin: vegetables, legumes, grains, eggs, muscle, organ meat
5. Riboflavin: green leaves, milk, liver, cottonseed flower, wheat germ, yeast
6. Vitamin A: greens, peas, beans, eggs, milk
7. Niacin: milk, lean meats, liver, yeast
8. Vitamin D: fish oil, fish liver, eggs, fortified milk
9. Ascorbic acid: tomatoes, citrus

Your German Shepherd Dog will be happier and his teeth and gums healthier if you give him a super-sized POPpup to chew on. Every POPpup is 100% edible and enhanced with dog-friendly ingredients. You can even microwave a POPpup to turn it into a huge crackly treat.

fruits, raw cabbage
10. Iron, calcium, and phosphorus: milk, dairy products, vegetables, eggs, soybeans, bone marrow, blood, liver, oatmeal

The primary objective for purchasing a dry meal is that the mixing of the products in the amounts that make the diet bal-anced ends up in a bag that is convenient to carry away. Commercially manufactured feeds accomplish this in many ways, which save owners the trouble of having to learn how to become a chemist and a nutritional expert. Not all dog foods are the same but a good rule of thumb to use when selecting a dry meal is to remember that...quality feeds need no supplementation. Many breeders still believe that because their dogs are growing they need supplements of calcium, pet vitamins, oil for the coat, etc.

Nothing could be further from the truth. Good quality dry feeds do not need added items to enhance the quality of a growing pup. The practice of supplementing the diet of a German Shepherd puppy only increases the risk of altering its natural growth and development patterns.

Research shows that the quality dog foods are directly related to their price. That doesn't mean that the most expensive product is the best one, but it does mean that among the many good quality feeds available, the manufacturers have formulated their products to meet the specific needs and requirements of the dog. The active working dog and the couch potato do not need to be fed the high cost, high fat and protein dry meals. Research and experience by breeders confirm that the supplementation of good dry meals, over feeding, excessive exercise and weight are the factors that interfere with proper growth and development. The simple rules that work are:

• Avoid supplements, unless they are specifically recommended by a veterinarian to correct a condition.

• Keep your pup looking lean.

• Table scraps should be fed sparingly.

• If your dog is a good eater and easy to keep, give him only small portions of the leftovers.

• The diets of good eaters can be varied to a greater degree without unfavorable repercussions. The diets of finicky eaters need closer monitoring.

Water is one of the absolute nutritional essentials of the dog.

Your puppy's growth and development are directly related to his diet. Be certain to provide a diet that meets your pup's nutritional needs.

Consider the fact that the dog's body is approximately 70 percent water. Its body tissues and organs cannot function without a regular supply of water which is needed to flush the system, stimulate gastric juices, bring about better appetite and act as a solvent

On outings and day trips it is important to stop and give your Shepherd a fresh cool drink of water.

within the body. When a dog is kept from water for any appreciable length of time, dehydration occurs. This is a serious condition for the canine which can lead to nausea, disease and body shrinkage. Water is the cheapest part of the diet.

Feeding Techniques

There is no longer the need for owners to prepare the daily meal for their dog to eat and it is best not to serve the food in a sloppy mixture, except in the case of very young puppies. It is better to feed the same basic ration every meal. Your Shepherd does not need a varied diet the way you do, nor is it a good practice to vary the daily diet. Food

Dogs have very sensitive digestive systems and should not be fed human foods. A sip of water would surely be better to quench this Shepherd's thirst than a soft drink.

should never be left out in the feed pan for more than 30 minutes. Dogs that do not eat their meal in that period are not hungry. If it has not been eaten by then, remove the food until the next regular feeding. If you allow them to have a second and third chance, they will become picky eaters. These spoiled eaters will learn to refuse food for two to three days until they are given exactly what they want. Remember, your German Shepherd is not a lap dog, it is a big and powerful working dog and should not be babied. If you have several dogs, separate them at meal time, which will eliminate the danger of finicky eaters being pushed aside.

Regardless of the diet or the feeding schedule always have plenty of fresh water in a clean bowl available.

Palatability and digestibility are terms used by nutritionists to determine whether the dog will eat the food offered, and whether the nutrients in that food are being efficiently utilized by the dog. When it comes to puppies, think of them as children. They are growing machines who need extra fuel to help them grow and develop. A good rule to follow is that during the first few weeks of life, pups need to be gradually introduced to solid food. Encouraging them to eat early by dunking their face in milk and cereal can be harmful. Newborn pups develop the muscle contractions of their esophagus as they develop. Early dunking of their face in milk and soft foods, to get them to eat early, can cause food to lodge in small pouches in the walls of the esophagus. Over time these pouches will stretch and may result in permanent damage to the area. Nature has designed the pup so that its esophagus develops the muscular contractions needed to handle food, as the weaning process comes to a conclusion.

The average adult weighs about 70 to 90 pounds, when fully grown, and will eat about 35 to 40 pounds of dry meal a month.

The question of how much to feed is best answered this way: if the pup looks a little thin, you are feeding it enough; if it looks well fed you are over feeding. The same can be said for adults. German Shepherds, like other fast growing breeds, grow and develop best if they are kept lean until skeletal development is completed. For most, this process will continue until about 13 months of age.

Puppies need extra fuel to help them grow and develop, however, overfeeding will only lead to a fat puppy with possible orthopedic troubles in the future. A good rule of thumb is that if the pup looks a little thin, you are feeding enough.

PREGNANT BITCHES

The feeding of a pregnant bitch should not change until after the fifth week of pregnancy. Beginning with the sixth week, the volume should be gradually increased. The size of her litter will not be influenced by the amount of her daily ration, because that is controlled by the genes at the time of conception. Usually two meals each day will satisfy a dam regardless of the number of pups she is carrying. As the pregnancy moves closer to term, the volume of food can be increased. Small amounts of supplements, such as 2-3 oz. of ground raw meat and cottage cheese with a daily vitamin, can be added in

There should be no change in a pregnant bitch's diet until the fourth or fifth week of gestation. The growth of the fetuses is small up until the middle of the pregnancy, after which it becomes rapid.

As soon as teeth can be felt with your finger in a puppy's mouth, usually around 17 days, it is safe to feed something other than his mother's milk. Puppy teeth are razor sharp and they will eventually become uncomfortable for the dam.

the final two weeks of pregnancy and throughout the nursing period. Special diets are not recommended; continue with the same dry meal.

LITTER SIZE

The size of a litter is determined by the genetics of the dam, which negates the claims made by stud dog owners that their sire produces consistently large litters. Males usually produce enough semen to fertilize far more ova than there will be pups. But since the dam determines how many ova there are to be fertilized she controls litter size.

Factors That Influence Litter Size

1. Age. Older dams generally have

smaller litters.

2. Inbreeding. Over time, it tends to reduce litter size.

3. Quality and quantity of sperm. Abnormal sperm in greater quantities (detached heads, defective tails, poorly formed). This varies from sire to sire and can easily be checked by your veterinarian.

There are breed differences with re-gards to the number of pups a bitch is likely to whelp. Generally the larger breeds produce more pups than the smaller breeds.

There are many factors that influence litter size, however, larger breeds generally produce 6 to 12 pups.

Prevention and Cure = A Healthy Life

Every owner hopes that his dog will live a long healthy life. Nowadays, this desire is enhanced through careful selection of puppies and breeding animals, modern technology and veterinary care and the family's care and concern—all of which aid in prevention and cure.

Dogs today are so much more fortunate than their ancestors. Regulations which were originally passed to protect property, livestock and humans actually ensure a dog's safety as well. Licenses and the accompanying taxes provide shelters for lost or abandoned animals, and a tag may prove to be a lifeline to home. Because leashes and confinement are now required by law, fewer families allow Rover to roam the streets.

Many diseases commonly fatal in the early to mid-1900s are now prevented through inoculation. An old-time exhibitor understood that if he took his dog to enough shows, the animal would contract distemper sooner or later. It was common to lose entire litters to the dread disease, which plagued canines for hundreds of years. Now, thanks to nearly universal vaccination, most

Your German Shepherd Dog should be taken to the veterinarian annually for his booster vaccinations and a general physical.

breeders have never even seen a case.

As recently as 1978, parvovirus swept the canine world, decimating kennels. As with all diseases, it was the very young and the very elderly that succumbed in great numbers. Thanks to modern research laboratories and the pharmaceutical companies, preventative vaccines are now available.

GENERAL MEDICAL CARE

Before a puppy is sold, he should have received at least one full set of inoculations, protecting him from distemper, hepatitis (adenovirus), leptospirosis, parainfluenza and parvo.

Many breeders vaccinate against corona virus and bordetella as well. Among the puppy's stack of official papers that are turned over to the expectant buyers should be a list noting the ages when additional shots will be needed. Although the schedule varies from breeder to breeder, or one veterinarian to another, the following is an example: six weeks—combination DA2PP & Cv; nine weeks—parvo; twelve weeks—combination; sixteen weeks—parvo and rabies.

Before the puppy goes to his new home, he should be examined by a veterinarian and pronounced healthy and free of major con-

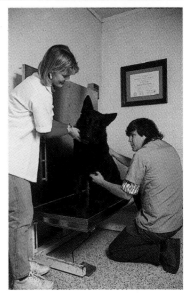

Regular visits to the veterinarian ensure that your German Shepherd Dog remains in the best possible condition. Your dog depends on you for his continued good health.

genital defects. Many, but not all, of the bite, eyelid, testiculate, cardial and esophagael problems can be detected before eight weeks, as can luxated patellas and open fontanels. From that

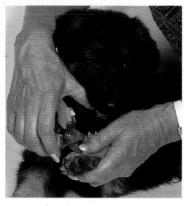

If you start trimming your puppy's nails at a young age and teach him to sit for this procedure, you'll have no problem when he is an adult.

point on, it's up to the new owners to continue examinations and veterinary care to keep him healthy. Routine health care, of course, includes yearly vaccinations and heartworm checks, followed by administration of the preventative.

GROOMING

Nails must be kept short for comfort. The toe nails have an inner quick, containing nerves and blood vessels, which grow with the nail, making them, more difficult to trim the longer the nail gets. Long nails are unattractive (forbidden in a show dog) and can actually curl around to cut into the foot. Nails that click on the floor send a signal that they are too long. Clipping them every two weeks will keep them short and neat in appearance.

Clean your dog's ears every week or two by using a quality product obtained through a veterinarian or pet supply store. Or you can use baby oil and gauze. Owners of longhaired dogs often pluck the hair from the inner ear to help keep it clean and free of impacted wax. This is not necessary with German Shepherds.

A dog who shakes his head or rubs his ear may have earmites or an infection, which must be treated by a veternarian. A red, inflamed or odorous ear also indicates a problem which should be treated by a vet.

DENTAL CARE

Dogs can't be fitted with dentures, so it's up to us to assure that their teeth last them as long as possible. Dry foods help

Your Shepherd's feet should be checked on a weekly basis. Burrs, interdigital cysts, or excessively long nails can all affect your dog's performance.

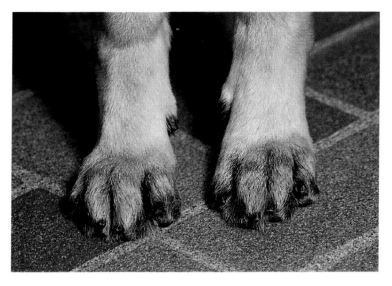

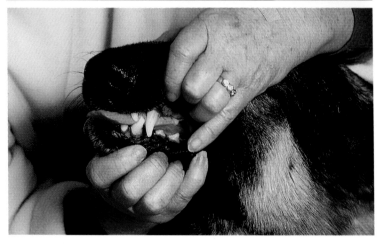

Your German Shepherd's teeth must be checked regularly for tartar build-up. At-home cleanings with a veterinary dentifrice should be done at least once a week.

the teeth and gums remain healthy. Feeding only moist or canned dog food can allow food to stick around the gumline, causing gums to become inflamed or teeth to decay. Even with a diet of dry food, tartar (plaque) can accumulate.

Cleaning our dog's teeth with a veterinary dentifrice, or a mixture of baking soda and water, is suggested and should be done at least once a week. The act of rubbing with a toothbrush and/or cleaning plaque with a dental tool is more important than the product used.

Never substitute your own products

for those specifically made for animals without asking a veterinarian. Human toothpaste or shampoos, for example, can actually be detrimental to your dog's care.

PARASITES

Taking stool samples to the vet should be part of the annual

The Plaque Attacker™ by Nylabone® has raised dental tips that help to control tartar build-up on your German Shepherd's teeth.

examination or when observing symptoms such as diarrhea, bloody stools or worm segments. Dogs, especially puppies, may vomit and lose weight when infested with parasites. Hookworms, roundworms, tapeworms, whipworms, coccidia and giardia are common. They can be eradicated with the proper medication but could be dangerous if left untreated. An over-the-counter drug may not be the right one for the particular parasite which your dog is harboring.

FLEAS

Bugs bug us and our pets. Fleas cause itching and carry tapeworm eggs. The resultant scratching can irritate the skin so that rashes and hot spots develop. Dogs lose hair, scratch and chew at themselves and are miserable. In attempting to exterminate the pests, owners tear their hair, scratch their heads, chew their nails and are also miserable. Better to prevent than to cure, but for everyone's sanity, once the invasion has occurred, the sooner the evacuation, the better.

Talk to your veterinarian about the proper products to use, then arrange a

Opposite: Outdoor areas with an abundance of trees and brush can be highly infested with fleas and ticks. Be sure to inspect your German Shepherd after inhabiting such areas.

regular reconnaissance to prevent a losing battle with fleas. During the warm months of the year, many people spray or powder animals (including other pets who may pass fleas to your dogs) once a week and premises (house and lawn) once a month. In between, owners keep up flea surveillance. At the slightest scratch, they look for telltale evidence— skittering teeny bugs or flea dirt, which looks like a sprinkling of pepper. It's usually easiest to see the free-loaders on the less hairy groin, belly or just above the root of the tail.

Many dogs have allergic reactions to flea bites. These pests can prove to be your German Shepherd Dog's worst enemy.

If your German Shepherd Dog does become infested with fleas, you can start by treating him with a good flea bath available on the market. There are specially designed products for puppies that are more gentle on the skin.

Among the products used to combat flea pests are dips, collars, powders, sprays, tags and internals—drops or pills. Instructions should be followed implicitly not only for best results, but because some of these products contain ingredients which may cause problems themselves if used carelessly.

If the critters are found, shampoo or dip all dogs (cats, too, with a product labeled safe for them), and spray living and sleeping quarters. It doesn't do any good to treat the animal without debugging the environment or vice-versa. One flea who escapes will happily reinfest all over again. If the infestation is heavy, it may be necessary to fog your house and to repeat the procedure a few weeks later. All animals must be removed from the premises for the period of time specified on the fogger can.

In addition to the regular regime, many owners spray before walking dogs in areas where they are likely to pick them up, e.g., woods, pastures, training and show grounds. Most flea pesticides also kill ticks, and daily grooming sessions should include running your fingers through the dog's coat to find engorged ticks. Natural, non-insecticidal products can safely be used on a daily basis in the ongoing war on fleas.

LYME DISEASE

One species of tick, *Ixodes dammini*, the tiny deer tick, is the culprit which transmits the germ that causes Lyme disease to humans and animals. Deer ticks are found on mammals and birds, as well as in grasses, trees and shrubs. They are rarely visible because they are so small (as minute as the dot above an i), but the damage they can cause is magnified many times their size.

Lyme disease can damage the joints, kidneys, heart, brain and immune system in canines and humans. Symptoms can include a rash, fever, lameness, fatigue, nausea, aching body and personality change, among others. Left untreated, the disease can lead to arthritis, deafness, blindness, miscarriages birth defects, heart disease and paralysis. In 1996, there were 16,000 deaths from Lyme disease.

People should cover themselves with pro-tective clothing while outdoors to prevent bites. Repellents are helpful for both dogs and humans. Examine the body after excur-sions and see a doctor if symptoms appear.

SKIN DISORDERS

Dogs, just like people, can suffer from allergies. While people most often have respiratory symptoms, dogs usually exhibit their allergies through itching, scratching, chewing or licking their irritated skin. These irritations often lead to angry, weeping "hot" spots.

During a regular veterinary exam, your German Shepherd will be checked from head to toe. Your dog's ears should be checked for waxy build-up or irritation.

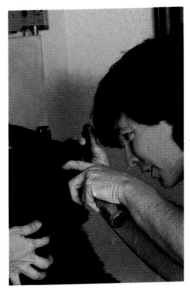

Responsible breeders screen their dogs for hereditary diseases. Be certain that the dog you choose and his parents have been certified by the Orthopedic Foundation for Animals.

Allergies are easy to detect but difficult to treat. Medications and topical substances can be useful. Avoidance of the irritant, is the best way to decrease problems.

CERF/OFA/VWD CERTIFICATION

Good breeders want to produce healthy, sound animals. The best way to do this is to start with healthy, normal animals judged to be free of hereditary conditions which can cause lameness, blindness and other disorders.

In the early years of dog shows, when symptoms of disease

appeared, owners asked the opinion of experienced local breeders and veterinarians. As time went on, more specifics were learned about these various diseases and their heritability. Veterinarians took x-rays, performed blood tests and more accurately diagnosed symptoms. Now we are fortunate to have experts in various areas. Due to their specialized training and the numbers of cases these experts see, they are more likely to be accurate. Some have formed organizations which register clear when tested animals and certify dogs free of hereditary disease.

Probably the first organization of its type, the Orthopedic Foundation for Animals (OFA) certifies dogs free of hip dysplasia upon clearance of an x-ray by three board-certified radiologists. Dogs must be two years old for lifetime certification. The OFA also reads and gives opinions on

A regular veterinarian cannot certify your German Shepherd free of dysplasia. It must be done by three board-certified radiologists.

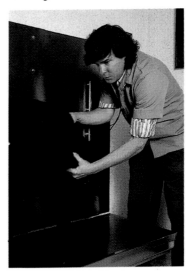

radiographs with evidence of other heritable bone disorders such as craniomandibular osteopathy (CMO), osteochondritis dessicans (OCD), ununited anchoneal process, Legg-Perthes disease and frag-mented chronoid process. The organization's address is OFA, 2300 Nifong Blvd., Columbia, MO 65201.

Eye problems can be detected by veterinary opthalmologists available at teaching hospitals, private spe-

The best way to ensure that your German Shepherd pup will be free of heritable disorders is to obtain a pup whose parents were free of such. Good breeders should never knowingly breed dogs that can pass along deleterious traits.

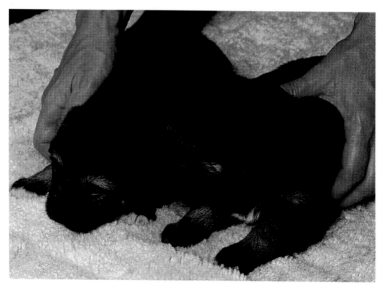

cialty practices (in larger cities) and at eye-screening clinics hosted by kennel clubs. These specialists examine for cataracts, entropion, pannus, retinal dysplasia, luxated lens, progressive retinal atrophy (PRA), central progressive retinal atrophy, Collie eye anomaly and other hereditary eye conditions. The Canine Eye Registration Foundation (CERF) may be contacted at CERF Veterinary Medicine Data Program, South Campus Courts, Bldg. C., Purdue University, West Lafayette, IN 47907. The age of the dog at first testing depends a great deal on the breed and the specific area of concern. A few diseases are appar-

To ensure that your German Shepherd is completely healthy have him screened for disorders other than hip and elbow dysplasia.

ent in puppyhood. CERF requires annual examination for certification of freedom from some diseases. DNA testing is now available in several breeds to detect with accuracy which dogs are normal, which are affected and which are carriers of these eye diseases.

Von Willebrand's disease (VWD) is a bleeding disorder

similar to hemophilia. Clinical signs include lameness, aching joints, bloody stools, chronic bloody ear infections or a failure of the blood to clot. A blood test measures for adequate concentration of a specific clotting factor. Although it may be conducted in puppies as young as seven weeks, it should not be done within one month of vaccination; therefore, most should be tested at five or six months old. If a dog is in heat, has just whelped a litter or has been on antibiotics, the test should also be postponed for one month. Other disorders have specific tests. Blood samples can be sent by your veterinarian to Dr. Jean Dodds, Veterinary Hematology Laboratory, Wadsworth Center for Laboratories and Research, NY State Dept. of Health, PO Box 509, Albany, NY 12201-0509.

Before you breed, it is always best to determine whether both of the potential parents are free of these and other hereditary diseases. Although the tests involve some cost, they are not as expensive as attempting to replace faulty pups. And they are certainly much less costly than a broken heart or a damaged reputation.

BONE DISEASE

Many canine bone diseases have gained nicknames—albeit not affectionate—due to the unwieldy medical terminology. For instance, canine cervical vertebral malformation/malarticulation syndrome is referred to as "wobbler" syndrome; panosteitis is shortened to pano; and canine hip dysplasia is often simply called CHD. The first symptom is usually a limp. Diagnosis is made through a radiograph of the affected area.

Craniomandibular osteopathy (CMO) affects the growth of bone in the lower jaw, causing severe pain. Spondylosis is the technical name for spinal arthritis.

Radiograph of a dog with hip dysplasia. Note the flattened femoral head at the marker. Courtesy of Toronto Academy of Veterinary Medicine, Toronto, Canada.

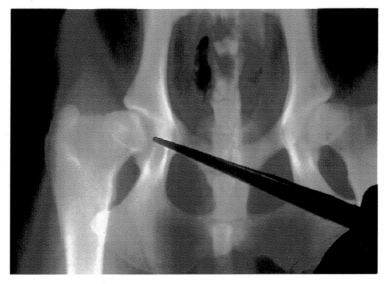

A breed as active as the German Shepherd benefits from exercise. If you suspect your dog to be dysplastic, limit his exercise time until you receive instructions from your veterinarian.

Hip dysplasia is the term used to describe a poor fit of the hip joint into the socket, which causes erosion and eventually pain. Wobbler syndrome affects the neck vertebrae, causing weakness in the hindquarters and eventually the forequarters. Osteochondrosis dissecans (OCD) affects joints, most often the shoulder, elbow or stifle. Ununited anchoneal process, commonly referred to as elbow dysplasia, is a failure of the growth line to close, thereby creating a loose piece in the elbow joint. Kneecaps which pop out of the proper position are diagnosed as luxating patellas, which are not common problems of German Shepherds. Legg-Perthes, most often seen in small breeds, is the collapsing of the hip joint. They all result in the same thing: pain, lameness and, left untreated, arthritis.

The exception is pano, which is a temporary affliction causing discomfort during youth. Pano may be visible on x-rays, showing up as a cloudiness in the bone marrow in the long bones, particularly in fast-growing breeds.

EYES

Entropion is a condition in which the eyelid rolls inward. Eyelashes rub and irritate the cornea. In ectropion, the lower eyelid sags outward, allowing dirt to catch in the exposed sensitive area and irritate the eye. In addition, extra eyelashes grow inside the lid which rub the surface of the eye and cause tearing. Either can be treated topically or, if severe, surgically. There are very few documented cases of ectropion in German Shepherds.

ORGANIC DISEASE

Heart disease affects

A canine ophthalmologist can detect cataracts in German Shepherds prior to one year of age. Cataract removal surgery is available and quite successful if needed.

canines much as it does humans. A dog suffering from a problem involving the heart may exhibit weakness, fainting, difficult breathing, a persistent cough, loss of appetite, abdominal swelling due to fluid retention, exhaustion following normal exercise, or even heart failure and sudden death. Upon examination, an abnormal heart rhythm or sound or electrical potential might be detected, or changes in speed or strength of the heart beat. Most heart diseases are hereditary, and affected dogs should not be bred.

Treatment includes first stabilizing any underlying condition, followed by medications, low-sodium diet, exercise restriction and, possibly, surgery.

Chronic renal disease may first show up in vague symptoms—lethargy, diarrhea, anemia, weight loss and lack of appetite—as well as increased thirst and urination. Kidney disease is more common among geriatric canines. It may be compensated to some extent through diet. Diagnosis is most often made through blood and urine tests.

GASTRIC TORSION

Because a dog's stomach hangs like a hammock, the ends are effectively shut off

***Opposite:** The health of your German Shepherd will show in his outward appearance. A shiny, glistening coat and bright, attentive eyes are good indications that your dog is feeling well.*

if it flips over. Nothing can enter or exit. The normal bacterial activity in the stomach causes gas to build with no release even through vomiting or defecating. The gas expands and, just like a balloon filled with helium, the stomach bulges and bloats.

Bloat results in physical torture for the dog and mental anguish for the owner who sees his dog moaning in agony and retching in a futile attempt to relieve the pressure.

With the veins and arteries to the stomach and spleen also closed off, shock sets in. The results are usually fatal. Torsion—medically termed gastric dilatation and volvulus (GDV)—is an emergency. Experienced owners, particularly of large breeds, know there is no time to waste whether it's the middle of the night, a holiday or vacation time. It is urgent to reach a veterinarian who can treat the shock, followed by surgery to reposition the twisted organs. During surgery, the veterinarian should be asked to tack the stomach to the abdominal wall to prevent recurrence.

AUTO-IMMUNE DISEASES

Auto-immune disease, like cancer, is an umbrella term that includes many diseases of similar origin but showing different symptoms. Literally, the body's immune system views one of its own organs or tissues as foreign and launches an attack on it. Symptoms depend on which system is the target.

For instance, hypothyroidism symptoms can include lethargy, musty odor, temperament change, decreased fertility or unexplained weight gain, in addition to the more suggestive thin dry hair, scaliness of the skin, thickness and darkening of the skin as well as chronic ear problems. Testing for hypothyroidism (which can be from causes other than auto-immune disease) may be conducted as early as eight to twelve months, using the complete blood count, blood chemistry, thyroid T4, T3 and free T4 tests.

Rheumatoid arthritis is a result of an auto-immune reaction to the joint surfaces. The resulting inflammation and swelling causes painful deformed joints. If the red blood cells are perceived as foreign invaders and destroyed, the rapid onset anemia (called auto-immune hemolytic anemia) can cause collapse and death if diagnosis and treatment are not quickly initiated. Often an auto-immune reaction in an organ causes destruction of that organ with subsequent loss of function. Auto-immune disease of the adrenal gland leads to hypoadrenocortissism (Addison's disease.)

The same reaction in the thyroid gland

soon has the dog exhibiting symptoms of hypothyroidism. Auto-immune diseases of the skin are called pemphigus, while those of connective tissue are termed lupus. Many other varieties exist, and each requires specialized testing and biopsy. Most respond to treatment once a diagnosis is made.

EPILEPSY

Probably because of the feeling of helplessness, one of the most frightening situations a dog owner can face is watching a beloved dog suffer seizures. As in people, epilepsy is a neurological condition which may be controlled by anticonvulsant drugs.

Many breeds of dogs have a hereditary form of epilepsy usually with an adult onset.

The University of Pennsylvania Canine Epilepsy Service has conducted studies of drugs and dosages, their efficacy and long-term side effects, to assist veterinarians in prescribing anticonvulsants.

ALTERNATIVE TECHNIQUES

During the 1970s and '80s, acupuncture, chiropractic and holistic medicine became part of the canine health picture. Veterinarians who have received special training in these fields now practice their techniques on patients who do not

Many veterinarians are specializing in alternative medical treatments. If your dog has not been responding to previously prescribed medicines, you may wish to seek out a vet who practices a new technique.

respond to or cannot take previously prescribed medical treatments. Patients have responded favorably to these methods, especially when done in conjunction with medical supervision. Certainly, when it comes to a much-loved animal, the most re-

The German Shepherd Dog is a hardy and long-lived breed.

Owners should be aware, however, that practitioners must have a veterinary degree to practice on animals and that the holistic, chiropractic and acupunctural treatment should not take the place of standard veterinary medicine, but enhance it.

GERIATRICS

As dogs age, problems are more likely to occur, just as they do in their human counterparts. It is even more important to examine your dogs, noting every "normal" lump and sag, so that if a new one occurs you are aware. Owners should make appointments for veterinary check-ups at least once a year.

cent up-to-date techniques should be tried before resorting to euthanasia.

Elderly canines suffer the same infirmities as we do when we age. Deafness, arthritis, cancers, organ disease and loss of vision are common. Symptoms such as a cough, bloating, weight loss, increased water consumption and a dry thin coat are warning signs to seek medical attention. Many aging patients can be made comfortable and sustain a quality life.

Although our dogs will never live long enough to satisfy us, we can extend their lives through our precautions, specialized nutrition, exercise and routine veterinary care.

EMERGENCIES

The get-your-vet-on-the-phone-drive-there-as-quickly-as-is-safe emergency situations are few, thankfully. But they do occur, and that's why all owners should be aware of symptoms. Veterinarian numbers for day and night calls should be posted prominently near the phone.

Occasions that are well worth a middle-of-the-night phone call are: shock, anoxia (choking), dystocia (labor and whelping complications), hemorrhage, gastric torsion, electric shock, large wounds, compound fractures and heat stroke. In addition, neurological symptoms such as paralysis, convulsions and unconsciousness

Your German Shepherd Dog is too precious to ever let anything happen to him. Have your veterinarian's phone number handy at all times in case an emergency visit is needed.

indicate an emergency. If your dog has ingested poison, been severely burned or hit by a car, for instance, call an emergency number for help.

EUTHANASIA

Most owners dread facing the decision of euthanizing a pet. But as hard as it is to make that decision and drive a beloved animal on his final journey, it is more difficult to watch a dog who has lost all quality of life struggle through a day-to-day fog of pain. Of course, it's also more stressful for the animal, and don't we love him enough to spare him that trauma? Certainly, eyes that plead "Help me" deserve a humane response.

Euthanasia is a fact that most breeders and pet owners must eventually face if they do not wish their animals to suffer. Ask your veterinarian to

Many German Shepherds live beyond 12 years and receive a certificate from the parent club called the "Thirteen Club" suitable for framing. The U.S. Military at the Lachland Air Force Base, Texas does even better. They begin working their German Shepherds at two, and retire them after 11 years of active duty. This serves as proof that careful selection and proper care will lead to a long and productive life.

administer a non-lethal anesthetic or tranquilizer, literally putting the dog to sleep while you hold your pet and caress him gently. The dog will drift off to sleep peacefully and without fear, no longer suffering. At that point, the veterinarian injects a lethal overdose of anesthesia which instantly stops the heart. Death truly comes as a servant in peace; euthanasia is a kind, quiet death.

Arrangements should be made for the disposition of the body prior to the euthanasia. Some owners wish to bury the remains themselves (be aware of local regulations, however, which are becoming more stringent) or to have the dog cremated. Others want the veterinarian to handle the arrangements. Planning ahead saves more difficult decisions during the trauma of losing your friend.

VETERINARY SPECIALISTS

With a surplus of small animal veterinarians expected in the latter part of the 20th century, and a surging volume of knowledge and medical technology, many veterinary school graduates elect to specialize with additional courses and training. These include surgery, dentistry, oncology, radiology, neurology, cardiology, dermatology, ophthalmology, theriogenology (reproduction) and internal medicine.

This "overpopulation," naturally, is a boon to pet lovers. If your dog has one of these problems, your veterinarian may refer you to a board-certified specialist or contact one for advice on specialized treatment. Any concerned, caring veterinarian will be happy to do so and assist his patient to live a healthier, fuller life.

Everyone who owns dogs for very long begins to build a canine medical chest. Basic supplies should include cotton, gauze, tweezer, ipecac, muzzle, styptic powder, cotton swabs, rectal thermometer, petroleum jelly, hydrogen peroxide, ear medication, anti-diarrhea preparation, ibuprofin pain killer and one-inch adhesive tape. Include first aid instructions and a poison help sheet with a hotline number.

ETHICS

In all diseases, symptoms may vary from mild to severe. In the most extreme cases, victims may have to be euthanized. Many do live, however, under veterinary care and supervision, occasional medication and owner TLC. Nevertheless, it's important to know which diseases are known to be inherited. Our dogs can

Responsible breeding efforts have led to decreasing numbers of dogs with hereditary diseases. This means that our dogs now have better chances of living longer and happier lives.

carry the factors which transmit hereditary conditions and pass on their afflictions to a higher than normal percentage of their progeny. Affected dogs should be spayed or neutered and never allowed to transmit their discomfort to future generations. Owners should also be aware that AKC regulations specify that surgically corrected dogs may not compete in the breed ring.

Canine Behavior

Canines have the same individual traits and quirks that people do. Each one is different. Although certain breeds have predispositions to the behavior elicited by their instincts and breed nature, every single dog must be judged as an individual.

Every breed was developed for a par-

Herding sheep and goats was the original purpose of the German Shepherd Dog. In this field he excelled as a competent shepherd's assistant and nighttime watchman. Today the breed's instincts are still very much intact.

ticular purpose. The best at doing their jobs were selectively kept and bred. Those that did not perform as they were supposed to were usually culled or, occasionally, given away as pets. The nature of the beast is predetermined by its ancestors—and by the people who bred them.

HERDING HEART

Born and bred to gather, herding dogs might round up children, toys or other domestic animals when herds of cattle or flocks of sheep are not available. The gathering instinct has been demonstrated by dams circling their pups to keep them bunched together or modern "shepherds" that chase cars or nip at the heels of the neighborhood children, who squeal their dismay at these natural instincts.

Cattle dogs and sheep dogs can trot tirelessly for an entire day. They accelerate as needed in short bursts of speed and high energy. As long as the activity includes their favorite person, they don't care if it's keep-away with a ball, fetch the stick or gathering the chickens.

Some herding dogs use the strong-eyed approach, staring their charges into submission and control; others are "huntaways" and bark directions like busy, demanding bosses. Yet they will-

At a trot the German Shepherd covers a great deal of ground moving powerfully but easily with coordination and balance.

ingly follow the directions of their superiors. There are many herding events spread across the U.S. each year. Those who own a German Shepherd can join a local club and enjoy the fun of taking their dogs to local farms and ranches for training. A herder's entire reason for being was, and still is, to serve his master and family; without that human contact,

As a herding dog, the German Shepherd's number-one priority in life is to serve his master—if that means playing a game of ball in the yard, he's thrilled.

these breeds some- times mourn themselves into a shadow of themselves.

CANINE ETIQUETTE

Good manners are appreciated whether human or canine. These start when we bring our pup home. The first thing on our mind is housebreaking. Housebreaking chores are made easier and speedier through the use of a crate.

Needless to say, the dog should always be confined to his quarters when alone. This avoids damage done to your part of the house through misplaced chewing or bathroom habits.

PUPPIES ARE PRIORITY

In the morning, the dog should be taken outside immediately

It is only good manners to train your German Shepherd not to jump up on people. You are responsible for your dog's actions—safety counts.

and praised when it does what you brought him outside to do. Then the pup can be fed and allowed to explore while the family

Crate training your German Shepherd Dog is the best way to be sure that he does not get into mischief while you are away from home.

When the first person arrives home, the pup should be taken out immediately, and praised when he goes. Following the necessities, he can be taken for a romp, fed, taken out again, then confined.

When the owner is at home, a schedule of exercising first thing in the morning, last thing at night, after meals and after naps can effect a housebroken toddler within a couple weeks. After relieving himself, the pup may be allowed freedom (preferably within sight) for 15 or 20 minutes, then confined again until time for his next outing. This routine should be continued for the first week or two—or longer, if necessary—until the pup has developed more

is performing their own morning routine. If no one is at home during the day, the little pup can be taken out one more time to do his thing and then put into his den with a toy.

bladder control and understands the intended routine.

Unless the pup is tiny, it's the middle of winter and/or you live on the 20th floor, it is best to skip paper training and go directly to outdoor action. If an accident should occur, a simple "No!" or "Baaaad" will suffice, followed by taking the pup out, praising if he manages to squeeze out a drop. Clean-up can be accomplished with any of the specialized pet deodorizers or with white vinegar and water.

TRAINING

Instruction begins at home, the minute we introduce our pup to his new quarters. In the beginning, it seems as though every other word is "No," just as when we are running after a human toddler. But, eventually, we can attempt various other preschool lessons: "sit" for a treat, "down" for lie down while brushing, "stand" for pretty, "stay" for a split second, "outside" for potty, and so on. The dog's vocabulary will increase though yours seems to have regressed. Before you know it, you will need to expand his education and yours. The key to teaching your dog a vocabulary is to only use one syllable words (no, good, sit, down, come, stay, stand) and the correct tone of voice. Dogs learn to associate the sound of the one syllable word with the command.

Most large communities have dog clubs or individuals that offer training classes. People who live in smaller towns or more rural areas may have to search a bit, but can often find trainers with–in a half-hour's drive. The time spent at classes is well worth the effort.

A good instructor has seen every problem in the book and then some and can give you the benefit of his experience. Someone has always walked in your—and your dog's—footprints, no matter how annoying, embarrassing or frustrating.

Obedience schools usually require that a dog be six months old or close to it. But there are other alternatives for early socializing and education. Puppy "kindergarten" is fun for everyone, dogs and people alike. Nothing is cuter than a pup, (except a bunch of pups) bouncing, bobbling and *boinnng*ing about. Even the most experienced owner is set back in finesse, while working with a wiggleworm, trying to avoid stepping on paws and encouraging acceptable puppy manners. Lessons range from sit, stand and stay (for the vet) to nail clipping, basic grooming, walking on leash and coming on command. It's fun and amazing how quickly these youngsters grow, from the tiniest Chihuahua to a mighty Great Dane, and before anyone realizes, it's time to go on to a higher level of education.

Conformation classes often accept puppies as soon as their basic inoculation schedule is in effect, or at about eight weeks of age. Training for the breed ring consists of walking and trotting on

Show dogs, like all other intelligent dogs, should learn the basic commands of sit, come, stay and down. They should also be taught how to heel on a leash.

leash. The pup learns to stand and allow the "judge" to pet him all over, look in his mouth and examine his testicles. Tips to aspiring handlers are given as well, allowing us to get our feet wet before diving into the big pond of dog shows.

If you are planning to show your German Shepherd, you must study the breed standard and learn how to show your dog to his best advantage.

Class training, whether obedience, conformation or kindergarten, teaches the owners how to become and remain the leader in this twosome. Just like a good dance team, one leads and the other follows. Unless we want a dog who demands us to fetch and cater to his every whim, we'd better learn to lead.

Instructors inform enrollees about the type of leash and collar to use, but most suggest a chain link or "slip" collar, with a leather leash. Probably 90 percent of the class simply wants a pet who doesn't jump up on everybody who comes to the door or can walk to the corner without tripping his owner.

Conformation training classes teach proper ring procedure. Techniques for setting up or stacking the dog as well as gaiting are demonstrated.

Class instruction includes basic obedience routines, which is also useful to those who wish to show their dogs competitively.

Hollywood dog trainer Michael Kamer works with a German Shepherd Dog off lead. It is always important that our dogs obey us even if we never intend to set foot in the ring.

Obedience exercises include heeling (on and off leash), standing, sitting, staying, lying down and coming when called. All of us can take advantage of those handy commands even if we never set foot in a ring.

How nice it is to tell a dog "Down" just as he jumps up to greet us with muddy paws or to say "Stand, stay" so that the veterinarian can examine him.

WHAT MAKES YOUR DOG TICK?

Canine body language can tell us what the intentions of the animal are and how we can greet the dog. A bow with tail wagging is an invitation to play. Submission to your will is shown by a lowered head, slinking movement and ears laid back against the skull. In extreme, the dog may lie down, roll over on his back or even urinate. Fear is demonstrated by a tucked tail, backing up, showing teeth and growling or barking. An aggressive dog stands as tall as possible, head high, tail raised, up on toes, ears and hackles raised, teeth bared, tense and growling.

FEAR OF PEOPLE AND OTHER DOGS

Whether caused by heredity or lack of early socialization, shyness is not desirable for dog or owner. Fostering social skills for a timid dog takes patience and time. Begin by boosting confidence at home. Give your pet a job to do and praise him when he does it. Pat him on the chest (in the ribcage area on the side) rather than the top of the head, which is a domi-

Obedience training classes are offered in most areas. Training your Shepherd is essential to your own happiness as well as the dog's.

nant action and increases submission.

Classes help boost confidence through consistent exposure to other dogs and people in a controlled situation. In training our dog to perform obedience or conformation routines, we gain more than a well-behaved pet. The dog learns that there is nothing to fear from other animals or from strangers.

Start slowly, if necessary, simply approaching other people while the dog is on leash and cannot escape. Continue talking to your pet and giving him praise when he shows even a minute amount of courage. He should improve with each day, although progress may be slow.

Walking the dog on a busy sidewalk or near a shopping center creates a situation sure to invite requests to pet the animal and draws people near for conversation. Tell the dog to sit and if you have taught him to shake, have him offer his paw. You've made a friend, and so has your dog.

AGGRESSION

On the opposite end of the scale, the dominant dog can also benefit from training which gives the owner control and dominance. Again, socialization, usually among understanding, tolerant "doggy" people, who know about aggression, can help a problem pup. If necessary, use a muzzle on the dog so

Walking your dog in public surely invites passersby to come near to you. Your trained German Shepherd must be always under your control, never growling, jumping up, or otherwise frightening strangers.

that accidental or purposeful biting does not occur. Once the biting habit begins, it is nearly impossible to stop. It must always be corrected and should never by excused.

With both extremes— the shy dog or the tough one—early repeated training and socialization are beneficial. "The earlier, the better" creates positive situations. Besides, it's

An aggressive dog may seem a viable deterrent for intruders, however, such a pet is unacceptable. Never train your German Shepherd to be aggressive.

a lot easier to train a dog that is small and still forming his habits than it is to force a large, stubborn animal who is set in his ways. Believe it or not, a mild-mannered, well-trained Saint Bernard is easier to handle than a panicked Min Pin or a nasty Silky Terrier who has never learned his proper place in the world.

Owners should be careful not to encourage poor character unknowingly. Often, people believe they are reassuring the shy animal or quelling the fire of a hothead by petting the dog and speaking to it in a soft, soothing voice. In reality, they're just fanning the flames, because these actions translate to the dog as "Good boy, you're doing the right thing."

Instead, the owner should make a leash correction and say in a firm voice, "NO!" and repeat the word NO, NO in a loud angry voice. Of course, aggressive tendencies would be curbed by a more vigorous yank and a louder tone than a "Don't-do-that" timid voice. Use

Aggressive tendencies should be corrected immediately with a vigorous yank on the leash and "No!" shouted in a loud, firm voice.

two or three repetitions if necessary. The word "Stay" can be used, as well, on a dog who has received training.

NIPPING

All puppies love to try their teeth on vari-

Puppies love to try their new teeth on anything available, unfortunately it is usually their owners' fingers and ankles. Try offering Gumabones® during their teething period to satisfy their need to chew.

ous objects, including their owners' ankles and hands. Although they're often innocent, puppy nibbles can turn into full-fledged adult bites, so it's best to stop before it develops into a problem.

A sharp "NO!" accompanied by a rap across the nose or squeezing the muzzle discourages most puppy piranhas. Herding breeds often chase moving objects, i.e., children, other pets, even owners, to round them up, and in doing so they sometimes tend to nip at heels or behinds. If this occurs with your German Shepherd, discourage the activity and direct it into the proper channels through instinct testing and trials.

CHEWING

Again, crating when there is no supervision prevents rather than cures. Pet shops supply products that act as an excellent deterrents to spray or wipe onto things you do not want them to chew. Tabasco sauce or liquid red pepper may also do the trick. Supply plenty of acceptable chew toys, such as Nylafloss®, Nylabones®, and other "pooch pacifiers."

Gumabones® will provide your German Shepherd with hours of entertainment as well as brighten his teeth and promote constructive chewing.

CHASING CATS OR CARS

Many dogs were born to chase and, in lieu of cattle, sheep, fox, wolves, pheasant or wild hogs, cars and cats serve as poor substitutes. Poor, because it's dangerous—to the cat, certainly, and even to the driver who may be startled into an accident.

Keeping your dog away from the road always helps. Setting up a situation in which you can make corrections sometimes works. Attach the dog to a long line and pretend to ignore him. When he succumbs to temptation, yank him as hard as you can. If he turns a backflip, don't worry, nothing hurts as much as being squashed under tires—or seeing the end come to your best friend.

Ask someone to be a co-conspirator and drive tantalizingly by, then as the dog begins to chase the car, correct him by shaking a can filled with something that makes a loud noise so that he becomes distracted and startled.

BARKING

This annoying canine communication may be the hardest habit to break, because it is in–grained in most creatures to create noise. After all, it's so handy, the noise-maker is right under our noses! Can you imagine a life without using your vocal cords?

Discouraging this neighbor-irritant is difficult if a chronic barker is the evil-doer. In those situations, it might be easier to buy the neighbor earplugs, or a good bottle of wine or his own noisemaker! But if the problem is serious, electronic bark collars or debarking surgery are preferable to poisoning or shoot-ing. Confining the dog indoors, particularly at night, can be a solution. Most people object more strenuously to night-time howling, yapping or yodeling, and who can blame them?

A monotonous lifestyle can be the cause of the canine complaints. The classic symptoms of boredom are digging, chewing and random barking. Give your dog something to do or wear him out, so that he sleeps instead of baying at the moon . . . or sun . . . or birds. Listen to what your dog is saying.

Unwarranted barking will not be appreciated by your neighbors and will give them cause to complain. Many towns have strict laws regarding disturbances from barking dogs, so damper your pup's barking from an early age.

Showing Your Dog

All-breed shows and trials offer a bit of everything. Each entry is a purebred dog of a recognized breed, and at all-breed shows, there may be as many as 130 or more breeds entered. Trials are for obedience competition and may be held in conjunction with breed shows. Specialty shows are for one breed only, and national specialties are hosted by the national "parent" club, usually accompanied by a great deal of hoopla.

Field trials, tracking tests, hunting tests, herding tests and trials and other instinct tests are usually held outdoors and are often hosted separately. Instinct, agility and temperament tests are offered as added attractions more and more frequently at large all-breed and national shows.

At one time, all shows were benched with entries tied to their cubicles for spectators to observe. Now, benched shows have declined, and few are still in existence. Every dog lover should attend at least one of these benched events, either as a competitor or spectator. Some exhibitors decorate their benches and spread picnic lunches on grooming tables. Since the dogs are required to stay on their benches for several hours, it's a good opportunity for showing off the breeds, sharing knowledge, making contacts, observing other breeds, talking "dogs" and having a good time. At other exhibitions, it's usually "show and go."

Competitive events are showcases for the breeders' best. Sometimes it's more fun to

Participating in dog shows gives you and your dog great opportunities to meet other German Shepherd lovers and to test your dog's training, good behavior and appearance.

observe, but true enthusiasts will tell you that when they aren't competing, they feel the itch.

As with any other passion, showing is a progressive disease. It starts slowly with a yen to have the dog behave and show well, to be in the placings, to obtain a leg or a point. Once that goal is attained, excitement mounts for the higher awards: Championship, a Best of Breed, a Group I, a Best in Show, Top-winning Dog; a High in Trial, a 200 score, an OTCh, Super Dog at the Gaines Classic; a field or herding trial placement, an instinct Championship, National Gun Dog Champion and so forth.

DOG SHOW MANIA

Most first-time buyers have no interest in showing. Oftimes the show bug bites the unsuspecting shortly after joining a training class. Following the initial exposure, the future show addict weakens and the "disease" settles in for a long-term stay and occasionally is terminal.

As the weeks proceed, we note how smart and/or beautiful our dog is compared to the others in the class. When a notice is passed about a nearby match, we decide to enter just for the fun of it. That's why it's called a fun match.

People go and have a good time, and so

do the dogs. The atmosphere is relaxed, other novice exhibitors and untrained pups are entered, and although winning makes the day even more fun, competition is not intense. Win or lose, those who have succumbed to the bug soon find another match or two and then begin thinking about shows.

Time marches on, and so do we . . . to the beat of a different drummer. Weekends are consumed by showing and doggy interests: conformation, obedience, field trials and instinct tests. Week nights we attend club meetings to plan these events. Our wardrobe consists of tweeds, mohairs,

washable suits, all with running shoes to match and with pockets for bait.

The family vehicle has grown from a sedan to a station wagon or van, and it bears a bumper sticker saying, "I'd rather be at a dog show." Realtors start calling about the five acres for sale just outside of town.

By this point, the enthusiast is eyeing another dog or three and planning the kennel building with indoor/outdoor runs. Often our first dog does not take the pro world by its ear, and we decide that ol' Phydeaux can enjoy life by the fireside while we set forth to search for the Wonder

Not every dog has the makings of a show dog. It takes a keen eye and a working knowledge of the breed to spot a "wonder pup" that will take you to the winner's circle.

natural instinct, a gorgeous head, superior movement, intelligence, and so on.

We know what we want—perfection. The trick is obtaining or breeding that ideal . . . or even coming close to it. That's what showing is all about: the quest for the ideal. To reach that unreachable star. It's not exactly tilting at windmills, because some come close—close enough to touch the star's tip, to be thrilled by its warmth. But perfection has not yet been attained. No dog scores 200 every time it walks into the obedience ring, and never has one remained unbeaten for its entire career in the breed ring.

Pup that stirs the judges' blood.

Depending on our experience and knowledge, we demand *top show quality* and qualify this with specifics: showmanship,

CLUBS

Joining a club is probably the best way to learn, advance and eventually help others attain their goals. Almost anywhere there are dogs, there is a dog club. More than 3,000 dog clubs exist, and these clubs host approximately 10,000 AKC-sanctioned events annually.

Clubs bring together people interested in a common cause, in this case, their dogs.

Joining a dog club is one way to learn about the sport of showing. Clubs host many AKC-sanctioned events, and these events can be both competitive and fun.

Whether we want to attain a conformation or obedience title, to breed better animals or simply to enjoy our canine companion, we can do it in the company of others who love dogs.

It's encouraging to have friends cheer us on in our attempts. Tailgate parties are more fun when friends are along, and when several club members attend a show, there's usually someone who has cause to celebrate.

Most clubs hold annual shows, matches and other doggy events such as instinct tests, seminars, demonstrations and training classes. A list of breeders within the club is made available to those searching for puppies or studs.

Most important, a club consists of members. Members who hold our hand when our pal is in surgery, who bring the bubbly when our dog finishes and who offer advice and company during a whelping.

It's having friends who help us through the hard times or who hold an extra dog at ringside. No matter what happens, someone has already walked in our shoes. When we come in fifth out of five, have a pup going through the teenage ganglies or own a bitch who has trouble conceiving, someone can usually console us and either offer advice or supply the name of someone who can. Being a club member means we can have company who doesn't care about dog hair in the coffee and who comes to visit wearing jeans already marked with paw prints.

Club membership is caravaning to shows, helping to tow another out of a mud-sucking field or jump-starting a battery on a sub-zero day. Members care about each other and about their dogs.

TRAINING

Training classes are offered through these organizations and by experienced individuals. Although it's possible to train a dog without attending a class, it's difficult to test an animal's abilities without distractions. With other dogs and people around, our dog may find them more interesting than our commands. But dogs have to learn to behave under any circumstance. Many an owner claims, "I can't understand it. He's does it all fine at home." The best learning occurs when the training takes place at different locations.

A class instructor knows how to solve a problem when teams are at a stalemate in an exercise and can correct us when we're doing something wrong to lead the dog astray. Besides, group training is more fun than doing it by ourselves.

Training is valuable for all dogs and all

owners, not just those who are going into competition. Probably 80 percent of all people who register for a training class simply want a well-behaved companion. The all-important bonding is intensified when dog and master learn to work together and develop respect for one another.

Training for the show doesn't stop with class, however. It continues at home, through practicing the stack, the stay, moving on leash, and through bringing out the best in our dogs by conditioning them. Repetition followed by reward results in the desired behavior.

Training your German Shepherd to be a show dog or simply to be a well-behaved companion will strengthen the master/dog bond. Cooperation and respect blossom together from a good working relationship.

CONDITIONING

Making sure our dog is in prime condition at all times includes training, exercising, grooming, instilling confidence and seeking veterinary care. Although it's best to begin exposing the dog to various situations by eight weeks, it can be accomplished at older ages if a newcomer to the sport decides to jump in.

A German Shepherd meeting another dog in the Canine Good Citizen Test. This test demonstrates the dog can behave politely around other dogs. To pass, the dogs should show no more than a casual interest in each other.

Professional breeders begin handling their pups at birth, gently touching, caressing and talking to them. As the pups grow, they are exposed to household noise and activity. No one goes through life tiptoeing about. Dropped pots and slammed doors are a part of our lives and our dogs'.

Nail clipping begins, as a necessity, at one week of age or the dam pays the penalty with painful scratches on her sensitive breasts. Breeders weigh each individual, while offering loving caresses. Setting pups on tables and gently brushing them is good practice for all dogs, show or pet, and should begin in small doses at five or six weeks. Pups should learn to walk on various surfaces—lawns, carpets and linoleum.

When the litter is about six weeks old, leash training can begin with pups following the dam or walking at will with the owner following them. After a few days of this, the owner can start changing directions, clucking and talking to the pups, encouraging them to follow.

Games such as hide and seek teach the puppies that owners do return, and a little later encourages the dogs to use their noses to find people and objects. Chasing a ball and returning it for more tosses introduces the retrieve.

As soon as the first vaccination is given, acclimation to crates and traveling can begin, heading for parks, training classes and other fun places, not just the vet clinic. Many clubs offer fun matches and training classes for two-month-old puppies. The official AKC shows are open to dogs at least six months of age and older. Even if the puppy isn't ready for serious competition, matches make excellent socialization opportunities. The most important thing for the dog—and the new owner—is to have a good time.

More serious training, accompanied by firm commands and gentle corrections, can begin as soon as puppies begin challenging authority, much like the human toddler. This occurs at various times, according to the individual. Some puppies are born angels. Most aren't!

Exercise at will is important from the beginning. Most dogs know when they've had enough. Road working to condition muscles or programmed jumping should not be undertaken until the dog is past puberty to forestall injuries to pliable growing bones and soft joints.

CONFORMATION

Exhibitors who like conformation showing champion the cause with gusto. It's more than just a beauty contest. It's an attempt to breed the dog closest to the standard, improving on each generation. It's being instrumental in the creation of a dog who causes a sensation, a murmur in the crowd... The dog who always draws the spectators and surreptitious glances from the judges in the adjoining rings.

It's handling that dog to countless Best of Breed (BOB), Group and Best in Show (BIS) wins, smashing records and setting new ones. And moving around the yard with a

A basic obedience exercise is teaching your dog how to walk beside you without pulling. This is known as the heel exercise.

We soon learn the jargon and doggy etiquette. Fifteen points make a Champion; nine of these points may be obtained in minor (one or two-point) competition. Two majors (three-to-five points) are required, and at least three judges must have found the dog worthy of receiving points.

Majors are do-or-die occasions because point shows require a larger number of dogs to be defeated than do the minor shows.

But all of this starts with a first training class, where the handler and the pup learn to walk, and then run, without tripping over youngster who never sets a foot down wrong and knowing . . . just knowing . . . that this is the one that will take you all the way, close enough to snag that star.

each other. Here the trainer teaches the handlers to bring out the best in their dogs and to look graceful while doing so. Some of us never attain this ability and hire a professional to do the job.

Handlers are convenient. Showing is their job, and they don't have bosses grumbling when they take time off work to attend events. Because they are able to travel and participate in more shows, their

Obedience training classes are offered in most areas. Dog trainer Max Lee and a German Shepherd demonstrate heeling at an obedience class.

dogs win more frequently. Because their dogs win more frequently, they attain more clients, and compete more often, and win more often. And on and on and on.

Breeders often have other commitments besides jobs. There are spouses, "What! You're going another weekend?" Children, "But, Dad, I wanna go to the beach." And whelping demands, "So you want me to cross my hocks until you come back, or what?"

Because handling is their career, pros have the experience and finesse amateurs often lack. When a person spends 40 hours a week doing something, he or she is usually more competent than those of us who eke out an hour or two of our spare time.

Occasionally, an owner doesn't attend any of the shows but sends the dog off with a professional until the Championship or honors sought are attained. Once the decision is made to hire a pro, we must decide who is the best for our dog. Most handlers specialize within a group or focus on just one breed. For instance, one person may handle all terriers, and nothing else. Another concentrates on "coaty" dogs, such as the Poodle, Bichon Frise and Pomeranian.

Find out who wins consistently at shows and ask other owners for advice. Observe, also, the handler's treatment of the dogs. Does the handler truly like dogs? Does the handler and his dogs look like a team when competing? Or is this only a way to earn extra money on weekends?

Ask to watch the grooming session. Is he thorough, yet gentle? Do his charges like him? Notice whether he is firm or rough in his methods. Cleanliness of facilities and exercise areas counts too.

Owners should be compatible with their dogs' handlers, and so should the animals. If there is a personality clash, someone's going to lose. Most times, it's the dog.

Ascertain the fees before making any verbal or written agreement to hire someone. A few professionals charge a higher fee per show, but cover expenses themselves. Most charge expenses in addition to their fee.

You may be able to share expenses if the handler has several other clients, but that usually means sharing time as well. Ask what happens when there is a conflict in another ring. Some handlers have assistants or work out reciprocal agreements with other pros.

Discuss all possibilities in advance:

veterinary care, bonuses for special wins, splitting of cash awards, length of commitment, shipping costs, entry fees, and so on. Even if you send your dog with the handler for a period of time, he should call regularly to let you know how he's doing and to work out further details. That's the meaning of—and the reason for—a professional.

Everyone has different methods of obtaining goals. With some, the game is incomplete unless they themselves breed, train and exhibit their dogs. Others are content with buying a superstar and cheering from the sidelines.

Still others fall somewhere in between. Whatever the route, the final destination is the same, to own a dog that excites the senses—and the judge.

For many exhibitors, the challenge lies at specialty shows. Winning under a judge who has a depth of knowledge about— and perhaps has bred, owned and/or exhibited—this particular breed is a coup, particularly when the win is over a large number of other quality entries. Gaining the nod at a national specialty show is especially gratifying. There will always be a thrill at being chosen the best among one's peers.

Most people compete at all-breed

shows frequently, however, possibly because there are more of these events than specialties. Here the excitement mounts as each hurdle is met and overcome: the class win, Winners, Breed, Group and ultimately Best in Show.

OBEDIENCE

Many owners sign up for a training class, hoping the results will give them a well-behaved pet. While discovering the yet untapped intelligence of our dogs, we yearn to find out just how good they really are.

German Shepherds excel in obedience competition because it is a breed who wants a job. The sport serves to satisfy that need. For many owners, the goal is to gain titles: Companion Dog, Companion Dog Excellent, Utility Dog, etc. Three passing scores (or legs) under three judges are needed for a title.

But a few hone the competitive edge, going for an Obedience Trial Championship (OTCh), as well as top wins in individual breeds and in all-breeds. To win an OTCh, the dog must garner 100 points from winning first or second placings in Open and Utility Classes against all breeds, including those who already have their OTCh. Capturing High in

Trial (HIT), whether at an all-breed, specialty or national show, is a coup that all serious competitors seek.

Special trials such as the Windsor Classic, the Gaines Regionals and Classic—which is considered the Super Bowl of the obedience world—attract the best working teams in the country. Amazing precision does not remove the obvious pleasure of the dog to be working with his best friend.

All of this brings the bonus of a good companion, one with enough manners to keep his nose out of the guests' cocktail glass and who waits politely for his own potato chip without too much drooling or too many mournful looks.

TRACKING

When it comes to tracking, our dogs always beat us by a nose. Canines have 40 times more olfactory sensory cells than humans do, and that's why they have such busy noses. Why not put to good use all that business of tracing down every crumb on the floor and sniffing at each other and visitors in embarrassing places?

Tracking, unlike the other performance titles, can be earned at any time, before the CD, after the UD or anywhere in between.

A dog's been using his nose since birth

when he followed it to his mother's table setting. Allowing the dog to do what comes naturally is not always easy for owners, however, because we're used to running the show. Training to track often consists of teaching the handler to "lay off" and to take directions from the dog, as well as steering the dog's nose in the right direction and on command.

The second hardest thing about tracking is forgetting about creature comforts. Tracks are laid in the rain, the cold and the heat, as well as on beautiful, balmy days. They're laid in muck and frost and amongst ragweed tickling our noses, as well as in lovely, grassy pastures. Over hill and dale in addition to flat surfaces. You get the picture—training must also be performed under such conditions so that the dog tracks during any trick of Mother Nature. Not only that, early morning is the best time to train while the dew is still on the roses. . . and the ground.

If you and your dog hold up to snuff and enjoy the great outdoors, then there's the TDX (Tracking Dog Excellent), and the variable surface tests.

HERDING AND FIELD TRIALS

Each of these have stylized the trials for the type of dog, i.e., spaniel vs. pointer vs.

retriever; shepherd vs. collie vs. cattle dog. In other words, a German Shorthaired Pointer is not expected to do field work like a Golden Retriever or an English Springer Spaniel. A Shetland Sheepdog works a flock differ- ently than a German Shepherd or a Corgi does.

If you like the combination of dogs and horses and you have a Beagle, Basset Hound, Dachshund or sporting dog, then field trials might be your bag.

J Rae Honey Bear O Firethorn moving sheep. As a natural herder, the German Shepherd always excels at herding events.

Although herding comes easily to a German Shepherd Dog, there is considerable training required to master this sport.

Locating and pointing hidden game birds are the object of this sport. Dogs (and handlers) must be steady to the sudden flushing of birds to wing and to the noise of guns.

Dogs work two at a time, in a brace, for up to an hour with handlers and judges following on horseback. When a point is made, the handler flushes the birds, the official gunners shoot the bird and the dog is sent to retrieve. Wins are judged on verve, style and stamina as well as manners. Field trials are also held on foot after rabbits for Beagles, Bassets and Dachshunds. Sharp working dogs may attain a Field Trial Championship.

Herding trials follow an obedience format, with three passing scores needed to attain a title. There are four titles which it is possible to attain: Herding Started (HS), Herding Intermediate (HI), Herding Excellent (HX) and Herding Champion (HCh).

There are three kinds of courses used in herding trials (A B and C). Each serves a different purpose and some breeds are more suited to one kind of course than another.

Cattle, sheep, goats or ducks may be used as stock in course A (for driving and farm/ranch dogs such as Australian Cattle Dogs, Bouviers, Corgis, Smooth Collies and Old English Sheepdogs). Sheep or ducks may be used in course B (fetching, gathering type dogs, such as Border Collies, Rough Collies, Beardies and Shelties). Sheep are used in course C for boundary herding dogs such as Pulik, Briards, German Shepherds and the Belgian herders. Each course has specific requirements, which include a level of difficulty, length and specific chalenge.

CANINE GOOD CITIZENSHIP

In an effort to promote responsible dog ownership and good

canine members of society, the AKC approved the Canine Good Citizen Tests in 1989. We have long since passed the time when dogs were allowed to roam at will—creating destruction, havoc and more puppies or alternatively being fed by the butcher, the baker and the candlemaker with benign good will. Today's dog must learn to adapt to modern, crowded society.

Dogs perform the tests on leash and are graded either pass or fail. The evaluators consider the following:

German Shepherds work in close association with farm owners.

1. Does this dog's behavior make him the kind of dog which they would like to own?

2. Would this dog be safe with children?

3. Would this dog be welcome as their neighbor?

4. Does this dog make his owner happy—without making others unhappy?

There are ten tests. The dog must:

1. Be clean, groomed, healthy, and allow touching and brushing by the evaluator who is a stranger to the dog.

2. Accept a stranger's approach.

The German Shepherd has a natural tendency toward protectiveness. These two Shepherds no doubt will prove to be this toddler's best friends. Lauren Nossett with her two dogs.

The sit and down on command requirement of the Canine Good Citizen Test demonstrate that the dog has been properly trained and will respond to the handler's command.

3. Walk on a loose lead under control—as though out on a walk.

4. Walk through a crowd.

5. Sit for an exam while a stranger pets him.

6. Sit and down on command.

7. Stay in position.

Additionally, the entry is judged on its reaction to:

8. Another dog.

9. Distractions such as loud noises, sudden appearance of a person or a person with an object such as a bicycle.

10. Being left alone for five minutes.

SCHUTZHUND

Some people think Schutzhund is aggression training. On the

Literally translated, Schutzhund means protection dog. It is a fast growing competitive sport in the United States and has been popular in England since the early 1900s.

dog is expected to search, find, guard and pursue a suspect, who is actually a decoy dressed in padded overalls and a padded sleeve.

The dog is also expected to protect himself and his handler during attacks. All bites must be on the padded sleeve and they must stop on command or when the attacker surrenders. There are many Schutzhund clubs in North and South America. Their objective is to foster protection tests that are intended to assure that the dog is neither a coward nor a criminal menace.

contrary, an aggressive dog is a detriment. One of the requirements is the ability to call the dog off a hold or "grip."

Schutzhund encompasses various tests, including obedience and tracking, as well as protection. During the protection phase, the

INSTINCT TESTING

During the 1980s, the American Kennel

Club encouraged getting back to the basics training with instinct tests. Their hunting tests began in 1985 and have been enormously successful, growing faster than anyone expected.

In 1990, AKC approved herding tests as a sanctioned sport. National clubs encourage natural instincts by sponsoring water tests for Newfoundlands, tun-

Schutzhund gives handlers and trainers a means by which to test dogs for correct temperament and working ability. In some countries, this test is necessary before an animal can be bred.

nel tests for terriers, lure coursing for sighthounds, coaching trials for Dalmatians, weight pulling and carting for working dogs, and sledding for nordic breeds. The only test for toy breeds at present is a daily one for all dogs—companions for their owners.

All of these instinct tests are pass or fail. Either the dog does it or he doesn't. This format is great for the pet owner who simply wants to see if his dog can do what he was supposed to do 100 or more years ago when the breed was first developed. The tests are also a way for the show exhibitor to prove

that, yes, his dog can do more than be pretty. Yes, he can work like he was meant to.

Hunting tests are divided into Junior, Senior and Master stakes with different formats for retrievers, pointing dogs and flushing spaniels. Basic herding test classes are divided into Preliminary and Principal. When the dog has passed both, he receives an HT (Herding Tested). The more complicated Pretrial Test shows more advanced training and a passing dog receives a PT (Pretrial Tested).

When a dog has never before been trained or exposed to

his erstwhile duties, it's amazing and exciting for owners to watch a dog "turn on." As the dog's attention is caught, his posture changes to one of alertness. Eyes become intense and muscles twitch in readiness.

These tests are also good news for the person who is non-competitive or has limited time or budget to spend on dog activities. Further information on these events may be obtained from the American Kennel Club, Performance Events Dept., 51 Madison Avenue, New York, NY 10010, and through books written on these particular subjects.

Yes, a dog can be attractive, conform to the standard and can still work.

AGILITY

Agility is almost more fun than work, and it's certainly fun for those watching it. Although a few people are beginning to take it seriously, most entries simply want to see if their dog can and will conquer the obstacles.

Originating in the United Kingdom in 1977, agility has become one of the fastest growing performance events in America. The object is for the dog to take on each obstacle as quickly as possible without making a mistake. These include jumps, a scaling wall, a rigid tunnel, a collapsible tunnel, a hoop, seesaw, wall, water jump and almost any other barrier a club can invent. There are also the table and a pause box, which the dog must jump on and then stand on top for five seconds before going on to the next obstacle.

The best time and performance wins. Relay teams increase the challenge and fun.

Agility, a versatile obstacle course for dog and handler, is a fascinating sport that is enjoyed by the participants and spectators alike.

Clubs may offer courses for large dogs and for small dogs. Agility is held as a non-regular obedience class under AKC rules.

THE INGREDIENTS FOR SUCCESS

Showing attracts young and old people of all shapes, sizes and ethnic origin, with their young and old dogs of all shapes, sizes and breeds. As in all situations, the human personalities vary, but the most successful dogs display confidence, enjoyment of the sport, and that elusive word "presence." Depending on the breed, a spectator might describe a dog as noble, regal, winsome,

The secret to success for German Shepherd ownership is togetherness. With this, the German Shepherd Dog can accomplish any task set before him.

To excel in any dog sport, both the owner and the dog should be enthusiastic and show a genuine love for what they are doing.

cute, amazing, smart or delightful. In all events, dogs displaying viciousness are disqualified and required to leave.

Both owners and dogs should possess and exhibit enthusiasm for their sport, no matter what the arena. If it's not there to begin with, it sure won't be after heartbreaking defeats, treks through blizzards and dropped majors. Sometimes even hundreds of blue ribbons can make you feel blue! Therefore, whatever the sport, the main ingredient is loving dogs and doing things with them that are fun for you and your dog.

Let's Play Ball!

When we're young, our imaginations can carry us to faraway lands, and we can pretend we're A prince slaying dragons, or cowboy, or ballerina, or whatever we want to be. Somehow, as we grow older, the magic of imagination fades in the face of the real world. We lose the ability to create fun whenever we wish.

We turn to material stimulation such as VCRs, HBO, RVs and ATVs for our amusement. Sometimes the

Exercise and companionship are two things German Shepherds enjoy. These three dogs are enjoying a game of catch in the snow.

best entertainment is the D-O-G lying right at our feet. One of the best reasons for having a dog is that they're so much fun!

When a dog owner wants to spend quality time with his dog, the first thing that comes to mind is tossing a ball or a stick. Oftentimes, the entertainment doesn't go much further than that and maybe a walk around the block. Even those recreational activities are better than none, but with a touch of our youthful sense of adventure, we can escape the humdrum.

TOYS

Dogs chew—especially puppies. Let's face it. When the eruption of needle-sharp puppy teeth stimulates the urge to sink them into something, better a toy than the table leg . . . or yours. Believe it or not, they really *need* to chew in order to develop strong, healthy teeth and jaws.

Chewing on some toothsome object also fills long, boring hours when the master is busy or away. Six thousand dollars later, after repairs to the family room, owners realize toys—proper toys—are less expen-

Opposite: *Your German Shepherd Dog will enjoy the Gumabone® Frisbee™. The Gumabone® Frisbee* has a molded dog bone on top which makes it easy for the dog to pick up if it lands on a smooth surface.*
*The trademark Frisbee is used under license from Mattell, Inc., California, USA.

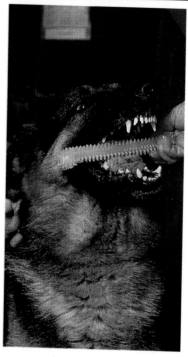

Raised dental tips on each Plaque Attacker® work wonders with controlling plaque on German Shepherds teeth.

Knowledgeable parents recognize that children's toys can be useful as well as entertaining. So can animal toys. Knucklebones obtained from the butcher provide exercise and chewing release, but can be messy. Prolonged chewing on these can also cause wear of the teeth. Rawhide products are popular but can prove dangerous if swallowed in chunks which can cause blockage in the intestines. All toys should be discarded when broken. A new toy is much more reasonable than a veterinary bill for surgery.

sive. It's always better to prevent bad habits before they occur than to try to retrain and repair and retaliate after the damage has been done.

Articles made from super-tough nylon and polymer (a soft rubber) are safe and good for dogs, and—as with nutritional, but good-tasting cereal for kids—your pet will never complain. Many are hambone scented and flavored.

Given one of these toys, old dogs seem young again in their play. Sedate, dignified dogs act silly. And young, silly dogs go "bonkers" for toys such as the Gumabone® and other "pooch pacifiers." The hambone scent probably has a great deal to do with the attraction for the

Preventative dental care is important in keeping your dog's teeth healthy and strong. Nylafloss® is an excellent decay-prevention device.

The Gumabone® is well liked by dogs. Available in three sizes to satisfy your puppy as well as adult dog, the Gumabone® will provide your German Shepherd with many hours of enjoyment.

dogs, but the long-lasting durability appeals to owners. Nylabone® products are also a big hit, at the same time serving as teeth cleaners and furniture-savers. When dogs need to get into some serious chewing, they grab a Nylabone®. These resilient, durable products, found mainly in pet shops, last at least five times longer than the cheap plastic or latex toys found at the grocery stores, and knowledgeable owners know they're a good investment.

When leaving the dog in his crate, a Nylabone® and a Gumabone® will make the hours pass more quickly until you return again to be the main object of his affection. These toys can be washed and sterilized, and they are non-abrasive.

The Gumadisc® is a flying disc, made for sailing in the air so that the dog can leap and catch it. Nylaballs®, too, are popular retrieve objects. Although their scent is unnoticeable to humans, it enables

All Nylabone® products are effective in fighting plaque and gum disease. Your dog's teeth will greatly benefit from constant access to a Nylabone®.

dogs to find toys hidden in deep grass.

Because dogs don't eat candy, they suffer few problems with their teeth. They can usually brag after a dental check, "Look, Mom, no cavities!" It's gum disease that plagues our canine

The nylon tug toy is actually a dental floss. These German Shepherd pups are happily playing with the Nylafloss® and benefiting from it as well. Never use cotton rope tug toys as cotton is organic and will rot. It is also weak and easily loses strands that are indigestible should the dog swallow them.

friends and results in tooth loss. Research shows that 90 percent of dogs over the age of three years are afflicted with periodontal disease. We can help our pets by brushing their teeth, scheduling regular examinations and by supplying good dentifrice toys.

Nylafloss®, particularly, is conducive to maintaining healthy teeth and gums. The nylon strands rub between the teeth and at the gum line, removing plaque and tartar, much like our own dental floss. Nylabone® products are sold in pet shops and by veterinarians.

The Tug Toy™ from Gumabone® is a helpful exercise device that can be enjoyed by your German Shepherd Dog.

Index

H-1062

The Book of the German Shepherd Dog

Anna Katherine Nicholas, 300 pages

PS-810

The German Shepherd Dog

Ernest H. Hart, 256 pages

JG-102

A New Owner's Guide to German Shepherds

Charlotte Schwartz, 160 pages, full-color photos

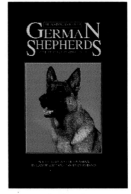

BB-102

Dr. Ackerman's Book of German Shepherds

Lowell Ackerman, DVM, 96 pages, full-color photos